EYEWITNESS ANTHOLOGIES

KNIGHTS & CASTLES

FAMILY LEARNING

This book has been specially created by Dorling Kindersley for Family Learning. The Family Learning mission is to support the concept of the home as a center of learning and to help families develop independent learning skills to last a lifetime.

Project editors Bridget Hopkinson, Phil Wilkinson
Art editors Ann Cannings, Jane Tetzlaff, Vicky Wharton
Designer Kati Poyner
Managing editor Simon Adams, Gillian Denton, Helen Parker
Managing art editor Julia Harris
Production Louise Barratt, Catherine Semark, Charlotte Trail
Picture research Kathy Lockley
Research Céline Carez
Consultants Peter Brears and Charles Kightly
Additional Photography Torla Evans, Janet Murray, Alan Hills, Tim Ridley, and Dave Rudkin

First American Edition, 1998
2 4 6 8 10 9 7 5 3 1

Published in the United States by Family Learning
Southland Executive Park
7800 Southland Boulevard, Orlando, Florida 32809

Dorling Kindersley registered offices:
9 Henrietta Street, Covent Garden, London WC2E 8PS

Visit us on the World Wide Web at http://www.dk.com

ISBN 0-7894-3790-2

Reproduced in Singapore by Colourscan
Printed in Singapore by Toppan

15th-century Knight's spur

Archers were used to keep enemies at bay

Knight chess piece made of ivory

Late 14th-century formal table knife

EYEWITNESS ANTHOLOGIES

KNIGHTS & CASTLES

A 14th-century
pottery pitcher

Different
kinds of
arrowheads

Written by
CHRISTOPHER GRAVETT and ANDREW LANGLEY
Photographed by
GEOFF BRIGHTLING and GEOFF DANN

15th-century Ornate
dining spoon

Floor tile from
a French castle

Medieval Gargoyle

FL
FAMILY LEARNING

Bodiam Castle in Sussex

Contents

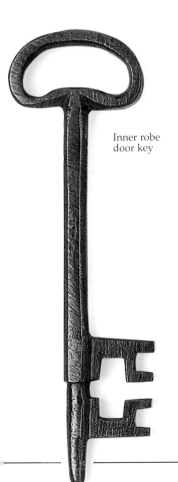

A 12th-century
Norman Soldier
bronze figurine

Introduction

This book shows what life was like in the Middle Ages – the period between the Classical Age of ancient Greece and Rome and the Renaissance. For 500 years after the disintegration of the Roman Empire, there were centuries of disorder, called the Dark Ages. By the eighth century, Charlemagne had united a major part of Europe and encouraged the spread of Christianity. After 1000 A.D., life in Europe became more stable. The Catholic Church was very powerful, and, in 1095, the Crusades began as a Christian campaign to drive the Muslims out of Jerusalem. During these centuries, magnificent castles and cathedrals were built throughout Europe. Together with Church officials, the land-owning barons and knights were at the top of the social structure. Knights not only defended castles from invaders, but they also fought to gain possession of the Holy Land.

Lead badge of a
king and his falcon

Castle window

Bishop's crook

Inner robe
door key

An Italian basinet
from the 14th century

The Middle Ages

THE TERM "MEDIEVAL" COMES from the Latin *medium aevum*, which means "the middle ages." But when were the Middle Ages? Before them came the Classical Age of ancient Greece and Rome, and after them came the Renaissance. The Middle Ages covered the period roughly in between, from the fifth century to the end of the 15th. In many ways medieval times seem remote and mysterious, peopled by knights and ladies, kings and bishops, monks and pilgrims. Yet European cities, states, parliaments, banking systems, and universities all had their roots there, and parts of the landscape are still dominated by the great medieval castles and cathedrals.

A LIGHT IN THE DARK
During the Dark Ages, art and learning survived in remote monasteries. This illuminated letter comes from the *Book of Kells* (c. 800), which was kept at St. Columba's monastery in Ireland.

THE BYZANTINE EMPIRE
When the Roman Empire split in two, the western half, based in Rome, declined, but the eastern half, based in the Byzantine capital of Constantinople, flourished. Its greatest ruler was the Christian emperor Justinian I (c. 482–565).

Viking brooches

SEA RAIDERS
The Vikings began to raid the coasts of Europe toward the end of the eighth century.

KING OF EUROPE
Charles the Great, or Charlemagne (742–814), united an empire covering much of modern France and Germany. He was a great Christian leader as well as a skillful warrior.

OTTO THE GREAT
The Magyar tribes that flooded into Europe in the tenth century were stopped by the German king Otto I (912–973). He became Charlemagne's successor when the Pope made him Holy Roman Emperor in 962. His realm in western Europe became known as the Holy Roman Empire.

THE DARK AGES
In the fifth century, the Roman Empire slowly fell apart as Germanic tribes from the north pushed across its frontiers, destroying towns and trade routes. Saxons settled in Britain, Franks took over Gaul (France), and Goths invaded Italy itself. In 476, the last Roman emperor lost his throne. These centuries of disorder became known as the "Dark" Ages, but this was not an entirely accurate description. Under the sixth-century emperor Justinian I, the Byzantine capital of Constantinople became one of the most magnificent cities in the world. By the eighth century, the great Frankish ruler Charlemagne had once more united a large part of Europe, encouraging the spread of learning and Christianity throughout his empire.

400–800

THE GREAT LEADERS
The Christian king Charlemagne supported the Pope as he tried to drive the barbarian invaders out of Italy, and in 800 the Pope crowned him "Holy Roman Emperor" in gratitude. Europe was threatened by invaders throughout the ninth and tenth centuries – Vikings raided the northern coasts, and the fierce Magyars pressed in from central Asia. But gradually new nations began to emerge. The lands of the Franks became France, Alfred the Great (871–899) defeated the Vikings to become king of England, and Otto I of Germany fought off the Magyars.

800–1000

NORMANS NORTH AND SOUTH
As William of Normandy (c. 1027–1087) was conquering England in 1066, other Norman nobles were carving out a large empire in Italy and Sicily.

THE CRUSADES
The Crusades (p. 42) began in 1095 as a Christian campaign to drive the Muslims out of the Holy Land. Jerusalem was captured in 1099, but later crusades were less successful.

German crusader's helmet

UNIFIER
This beautiful gilded head represents the powerful Holy Roman emperor Frederick I, or Barbarossa (1121–1190), who brought unity to the German states in the 12th century.

THE GREAT PLAGUE
The Black Death had a lasting effect on European society. So many peasants died that there were hardly enough people left to farm the land. Increased demands on their labor caused the peasants to revolt in both France and England.

Bishop's crozier, or crook

THE CHURCH
The Catholic Church was one of the most powerful institutions of the Middle Ages. During the 13th century, the religious Inquisition was established to hunt out those who disagreed with its teachings. Those found guilty could be punished with excommunication (being cut off from the Church) or even death.

RENAISSANCE GENIUS
Michelangelo (1475–1564) was one of the greatest Renaissance sculptors. His most famous work is the beautiful marble statue the *David*, now in Florence.

DISSOLVING THE MONASTERIES
When the English king Henry VIII (1491–1547) quarreled with the Catholic Church, he appointed himself head of the Church in England and "dissolved" the great monasteries, taking their lands and property.

PEACE AND STABILITY
After 1000, life in Europe became more stable. Supported by the feudal system (p. 32), strong rulers brought order and peace to the new nations. This encouraged trade and the growth of towns and cities, and the population rose. The Catholic Church (p. 36) reached the peak of its power as great cathedrals were built and new monastic orders were formed (p. 98). The first European university was founded in Italy.

PLAGUE AND WAR
The 14th century saw a series of disasters strike Europe. Bad harvests caused famine, and the Black Death (p. 62) killed a third of the population. England and France began the Hundred Years' War in 1337, and church leaders squabbled over the title of pope. However, there was also an expansion in trade spearheaded in northern Europe by the prosperous Hanseatic League.

NEW BEGINNINGS
The 15th century was a time of change. Scholars and artists explored new ideas and artistic styles in the Renaissance, and in the 1500s religious reformers broke away from the Catholic Church in the Reformation. This was also an age of great discovery. Explorers from Spain and Portugal crossed the Atlantic and Indian oceans, opening new horizons for trade and development.

1000–1250   1250–1400   1400–1540

The first knights

In the fourth century A.D. the Roman Empire fell and Europe was invaded by various barbarian tribes. One of the dominant groups was the Franks of central and western Europe, who gradually expanded their power until, in A.D. 800, their leader Charlemagne (right) became emperor of the West. Charlemagne and his forebears added to the number of horsemen in their army, giving land to mounted warriors. In the ninth century the empire, torn by civil wars and invasions, broke up. Powerful local lords and their mounted warriors offered protection to peasants, who became their serfs in return. In this feudal system, which first developed in western Europe, the lords themselves owed allegiance to greater lords, and all were bound by oaths of loyalty. All these lords, and some of the men who served them, were knights – warriors who fought on horseback. By the 11th century a new social order was formed by armored knights, who served a local lord, count, or duke, and were in turn served by serfs.

WINGED SPEAR *right*
Charlemagne's infantrymen (foot soldiers) usually carried spears with lugs that stuck out; but cavalrymen (mounted warriors) may have used smaller versions as well. The lugs could keep a weapon from sliding down the shaft, or prevent the spear from getting stuck in an opponent's body. They might also have helped if the spear was used for fencing.

CAROLINGIAN CAVALRY
Under Charlemagne and his descendants, the Carolingians, armored horsemen became more and more important. In this late-ninth-century manuscript the men have coats of scale armor, helmets, shields, and spears. They now ride with stirrups for a more secure seat. The man in front carries a dragon banner shaped like a wind sock.

Sharp, double-edged blade

Lug

Socket to insert shaft

BARBARIAN HORSEMAN
When the Roman Empire broke up, many horsemen from eastern Europe arrived in the west. This plaque shows a Lombard horseman of about 600. Unlike a later knight, he uses no stirrups or saddle, but horsemen like him were the forerunners of the mounted warriors of later centuries.

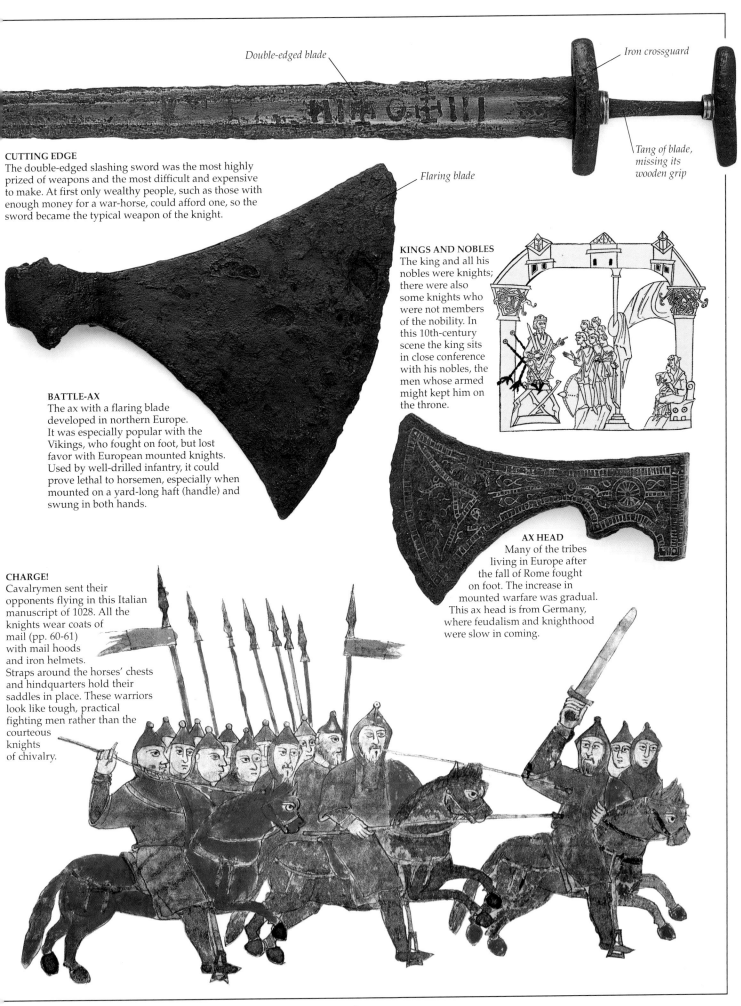

Double-edged blade

Iron crossguard

Tang of blade, missing its wooden grip

CUTTING EDGE
The double-edged slashing sword was the most highly prized of weapons and the most difficult and expensive to make. At first only wealthy people, such as those with enough money for a war-horse, could afford one, so the sword became the typical weapon of the knight.

Flaring blade

BATTLE-AX
The ax with a flaring blade developed in northern Europe. It was especially popular with the Vikings, who fought on foot, but lost favor with European mounted knights. Used by well-drilled infantry, it could prove lethal to horsemen, especially when mounted on a yard-long haft (handle) and swung in both hands.

KINGS AND NOBLES
The king and all his nobles were knights; there were also some knights who were not members of the nobility. In this 10th-century scene the king sits in close conference with his nobles, the men whose armed might kept him on the throne.

AX HEAD
Many of the tribes living in Europe after the fall of Rome fought on foot. The increase in mounted warfare was gradual. This ax head is from Germany, where feudalism and knighthood were slow in coming.

CHARGE!
Cavalrymen sent their opponents flying in this Italian manuscript of 1028. All the knights wear coats of mail (pp. 60-61) with mail hoods and iron helmets. Straps around the horses' chests and hindquarters hold their saddles in place. These warriors look like tough, practical fighting men rather than the courteous knights of chivalry.

The first castles

M ANY OF THE GREAT fortifications of the Middle Ages are standing today, still dominating the surrounding countryside. Why were they originally built and who lived in them? A castle was the fortified private residence of a lord. The lord could be a king or a lesser baron, but in either case the castle was a home as well as a stronghold. A castle was designed to be safe against the cavalry charge of knights, so safe that it could withstand a lengthy assault or siege by an enemy. A castle was also a community with many staff: the constable or castellan looked after the buildings and defenses; the marshal was in charge of the horses, garrison, and outside servants; the chamberlain oversaw food and drink; and the steward ran the estates and finances.

TALL TOWERS
San Gimignano, Italy, is an extreme example of what happened when rival families clashed. Here 72 tall castles were built in the same town, of which 14 survive today.

OLD AND NEW
Castle walls or buildings were often repaired or replaced, to take advantage of new defensive ideas. At Falaise, France, the castle was given a square tower by Henry I in the 12th century and a round one by King Philip Augustus in the early 13th century.

ANCESTOR
At Mycenae, Greece, a strong fortified palace was built in about 1250 B.C. The Lion Gate guards the entrance. Such a state-run building is not a true castle, even though it has large stone fortifications.

IRON AGE
The large earthworks at Maiden castle, England, are actually the remains of a Celtic palisaded (fenced) settlement built on a New Stone Age site. It was really more like a fortified town than a castle and was captured by the Romans.

Natural rocky outcrop provides base for castle

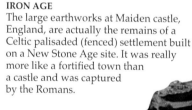

MASTER

This early 14th-century picture shows a king instructing a master mason, who was in charge of the castle's construction. He carries a set square. Some kings built numerous castles but lived in them only occasionally.

SYMBOL OF POWER

As well as being a home, the castle was a symbol of power. Caernarfon in North Wales, begun together with a walled town in 1283, was one of a series of castles built by Edward I of England in order to impress the people of Wales.

Main stone tower on top of mound

Inner curtain wall

TURKISH TOWERS

Van castle in Turkey was begun in A.D. 850. During the Middle Ages it was repaired by the Seljuk and Ottoman Turks, and was later lived in by Armenian Christians.

Steep crag makes castle difficult to attack

MEETING PLACE

Castles were often the scenes of important meetings about state affairs. This picture shows the meeting of Richard II and his uncle the Duke of Gloucester that took place at Pleshey castle.

Kinds of castle

A CASTLE COULD BE a lord's private home and his business headquarters, as well as a base for his soldiers. The first castles probably appeared in northwestern France in the ninth century, because of civil wars and Viking attacks. Although some early castles were built of stone, many consisted of earthworks and timber walls. But slowly knights began to build castles of stone and later brick, because these materials were stronger and more fire-resistant. In the late 15th century, more settled societies, demand for comfort, and the increasing use of powerful cannons meant that castles became less important. Some of their military roles were taken over by forts, defended gun platforms controlled by the state.

NARROW SLIT
Windows near the ground were made very small to guard against enemy missiles or soldiers climbing through. Such windows were narrow on the outside but splayed on the inside to let in as much light as possible.

MOTTE AND BAILEY
The castles of the 10th to 12th centuries usually consisted of a ditch and rampart with wooden fences. From the 11th century on, many were also given a mound called a motte, a last line of defense with a wooden tower on top. The bailey, or courtyard, below it held all the domestic buildings.

STRENGTH IN STONE
Stone donjons, or keeps, became common in the late 11th and 12th centuries. The larger ones could hold accommodation for the lord and his household. The bailey was by now often surrounded by stone walls with square towers. Round towers appeared in the 12th century.

RINGS OF DEFENSE
Concentric castles, which were first built in the 13th century, had two rings of walls, one within the other. This gave two lines of defence. The inner ring was often higher to give archers a clear field of fire. Some old castles with keeps had outer rings, added later; these gave yet another line of defense. Sometimes rivers were used to give broad water defenses.

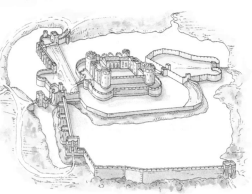

MEN AT WORK
Stone castles cost a fortune to build and could take years to complete. The lord and the master mason chose a strong site and plan. Stone had to be brought in specially. In addition, large amounts of lime, sand, and water were needed for the mortar. The materials and work force were normally provided by the lord.

CRACKING CASTLE
Sometimes wooden fences on the motte were replaced by stone walls, forming a shell keep. Occasionally a stone tower was built on a motte, but the artificial mound was not always strong enough to take the weight. The 13th-century Clifford's Tower in York, England, has cracked as a result.

GATEHOUSE
Castle gatehouses were always strongly fortified. At Dover, England, the gate is flanked by two massive round towers. The walls are splayed at the base; the thicker masonry helps to protect them against mining. There is also a deep dry ditch to obstruct attackers.

INSIDE A KEEP
A large keep like the one at Rochester had enough space to house the lord and his followers. The basement was used for storage. The first floor usually housed the garrison. The hall on the next floor was used by everyone to eat and in some cases sleep in. The lord's family had rooms on the top floor of the keep.

Wooden hoarding to allow soldiers to overlook the base of the wall

Chapel

Spiral stone stairs

Lord's apartments

Great hall

Guardrooms

Storerooms

GOOD SITE
This view of the keep at Rochester shows how it is surrounded by strong outer defensive walls.

A GREAT TOWER
The keep, or donjon (from which comes the English word "dungeon", an underground prison), always had strong walls. At Rochester, begun in 1087, they are 12 ft (3.7 m) thick at the base and the tower is 70 ft (21 m) high. The entrance was always on the first floor and was often protected by a forebuilding. There was a well in the basement, to provide water if the garrison was trapped in the tower during a siege.

Merlon or battlement

Corner turret

Buttress to strengthen wall

Large upper window later made even larger

Merlon in forebuilding

Chapel window

Forebuilding with entrance doorway

Drawbridge pit

Narrow slit on lower level, to protect against enemy missiles

Motte-and-Bailey

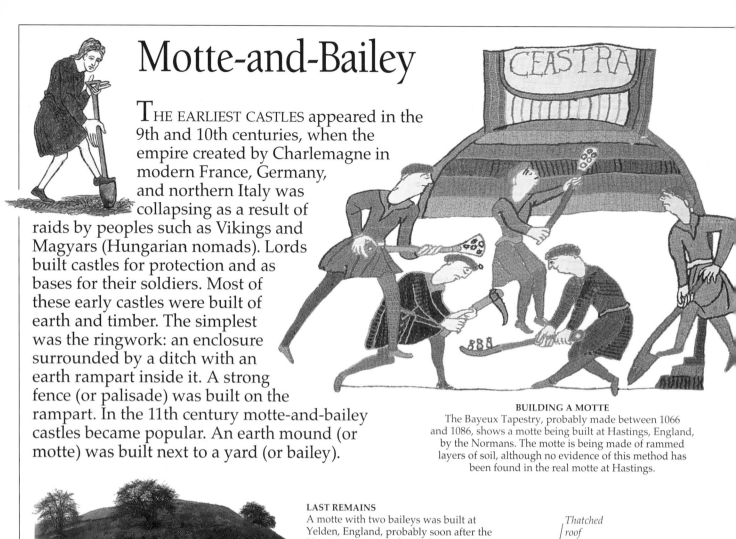

THE EARLIEST CASTLES appeared in the 9th and 10th centuries, when the empire created by Charlemagne in modern France, Germany, and northern Italy was collapsing as a result of raids by peoples such as Vikings and Magyars (Hungarian nomads). Lords built castles for protection and as bases for their soldiers. Most of these early castles were built of earth and timber. The simplest was the ringwork: an enclosure surrounded by a ditch with an earth rampart inside it. A strong fence (or palisade) was built on the rampart. In the 11th century motte-and-bailey castles became popular. An earth mound (or motte) was built next to a yard (or bailey).

BUILDING A MOTTE
The Bayeux Tapestry, probably made between 1066 and 1086, shows a motte being built at Hastings, England, by the Normans. The motte is being made of rammed layers of soil, although no evidence of this method has been found in the real motte at Hastings.

LAST REMAINS
A motte with two baileys was built at Yelden, England, probably soon after the Norman conquest. The ditches were fed by a local stream. Often a grassy mound like this is all that remains of an early castle.

Lifting bridge

Wood palisade

Stables

Thatched roof

Hall

Bailey

Castle yard or bailey

Earth motte

TIMBER TOWER
This stylized picture of a motte comes from the Bayeux Tapestry. It is supposed to show the castle at Rennes, the former capital of Brittany. The wooden palisade around the top encloses a wooden tower. If it were not for pictures like this, we would not know what these towers looked like.

PLESHEY
The large motte-and-bailey at Pleshey, England, was built by the Normans soon after 1066. This type of castle could be erected in a matter of months rather than years, which was ideal when the Normans were in a hostile country. Pleshey castle has one motte and one bailey, but sometimes there were two mottes or two baileys.

Roof of wooden shingles

Wood stilts to give space under tower

MOTTE-AND-BAILEY STYLE
These castles were built in the 11th and 12th centuries. There was a bailey or courtyard, protected by a ditch and palisade, and an entrance gate often with a lifting bridge, a drawbridge, or even a gate tower. Within the bailey were stables and workshops, a well, and perhaps a chapel. The motte was the final refuge. Many mottes were only about 15 ft (5 m) high, but some were twice that size. The tower on top was usually of wood – stone towers were often too heavy for artificial mounds. Some towers had many rooms, but if there was only space for a watchtower on the motte, a great hall might be built in the bailey.

Wooden walkway

Motte, or earth mound

Wooden flying (overhead) bridge

The great tower

DURING THE 10TH CENTURY lords began to build castles out of stone. A large stone tower could become the main military and residential building of a castle. Because the towers were expensive to build and took a long time to erect, and because skilled masons (stoneworkers) were needed to plan and build them, few such towers were built until the 11th century. They are now often known as keeps, but in their day they were called great towers or donjons. The Normans liked great towers with massively thick stone walls, and they built several after their conquest of England in 1066. Many more were built in the next century. Stone towers were stronger than wooden walls and did not burn. Attackers had to use other ways to destroy them, such as chipping away at the corners with picks, or digging tunnels beneath (undermining) the foundations to weaken them.

PRISON
Great towers had many different uses. Here the Duke of Orleans, captured by the English at the Battle of Agincourt in 1415, awaits his ransom. He is held in the White Tower, in the middle of the Tower of London.

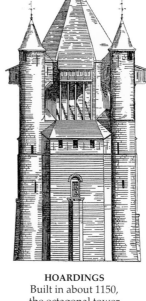

HOARDINGS
Built in about 1150, the octagonal tower at Provins, France, is shown here with wooden hoardings (pp. 86-87) that were added later.

SHELL
As stone defenses became more common, the wooden palisades around the top of a motte (pp. 14–15) were sometimes replaced with stone walls for added strength. Structures like this are now called shell keeps. This ring-work (low stone wall) at Restormel, Cornwall, also has low stone walls and provides a roomy courtyard within the walls.

Double windows provide more light

GREAT HALL
One floor of the great tower of Hedingham castle was used as the great hall, in which the lord and his household lived and ate. To light the hall, large alcoves were set into the walls. Doors in some of the alcoves lead to lavatories or rooms called mural chambers. The level above has a gallery recessed into the wall, and it runs the length of the hall.

Window in alcove

Zigzag decoration, typical of buildings of the 12th century

KEEPING WARM
In wooden buildings the fire was made in an open hearth in the middle of the floor. But with a stone tower fireplaces could be built into the thickness of the wall. The flue passed through the wall to the outside and carried much of the smoke away from the room.

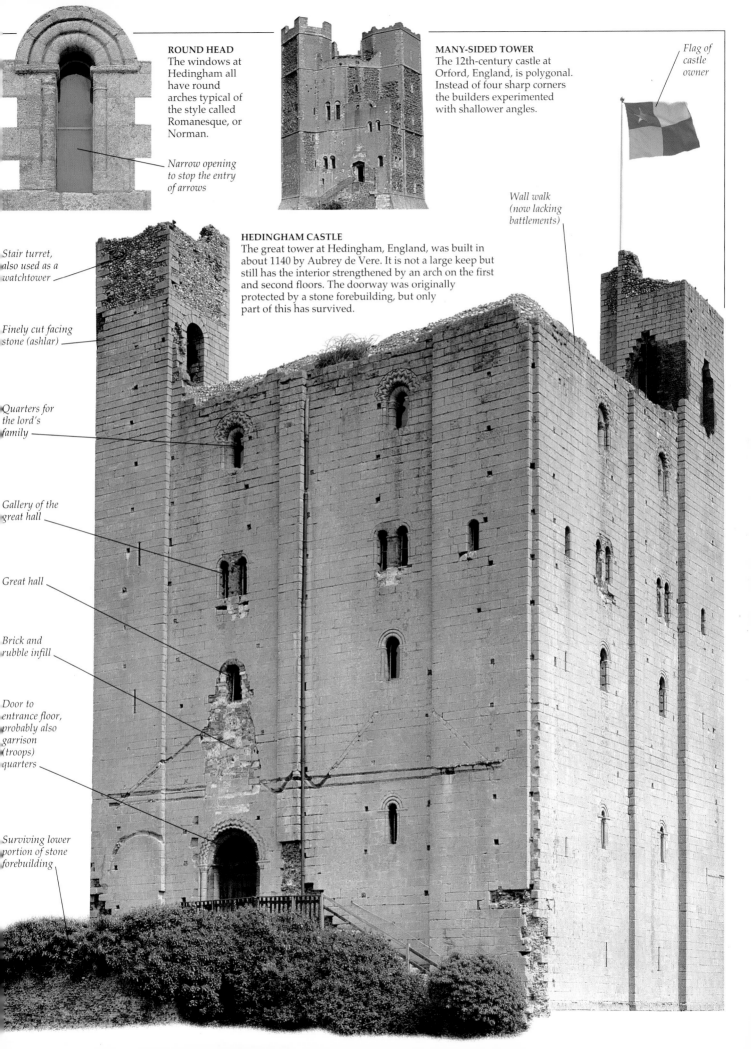

ROUND HEAD
The windows at Hedingham all have round arches typical of the style called Romanesque, or Norman.

Narrow opening to stop the entry of arrows

MANY-SIDED TOWER
The 12th-century castle at Orford, England, is polygonal. Instead of four sharp corners the builders experimented with shallower angles.

Flag of castle owner

Wall walk (now lacking battlements)

HEDINGHAM CASTLE
The great tower at Hedingham, England, was built in about 1140 by Aubrey de Vere. It is not a large keep but still has the interior strengthened by an arch on the first and second floors. The doorway was originally protected by a stone forebuilding, but only part of this has survived.

Stair turret, also used as a watchtower

Finely cut facing stone (ashlar)

Quarters for the lord's family

Gallery of the great hall

Great hall

Brick and rubble infill

Door to entrance floor, probably also garrison (troops) quarters

Surviving lower portion of stone forebuilding

Concentric castles

CONQUERING KING
Edward I was a great builder of castles in North Wales.

Fʀᴏᴍ ᴛʜᴇ ᴍɪᴅ 13ᴛʜ ᴄᴇɴᴛᴜʀʏ, castles were built with rings of stone walls, one inside the other. These are called concentric castles. The outer wall was fairly close to and lower than the inner, sometimes so low that it seemed no more than a barrier against siege machines (such as catapults). But it meant that archers on the inner walls could shoot over the heads of those on the outer, bringing twice the fire power to bear on an enemy. If attackers broke through the outer wall, they would still be faced with the inner wall. Some towers could be sealed off, leaving the enemy exposed on the wall walks of the outer wall. In older castles the great tower and curtain wall were sometimes given an outer ring of walls, making three lines of defense.

GATEHOUSE
This is the gatehouse on a dam wall which leads to the outer eastern gate at Caerphilly castle. The twin holes above the archway are for the chains of a lifting bridge. Behind this were a portcullis and double-doors. Notice the "spurs" which jut out to strengthen the base of each tower.

Round corner tower

Putlog holes to take wood supports for hoardings

Gatehouse

Outer curtain wall

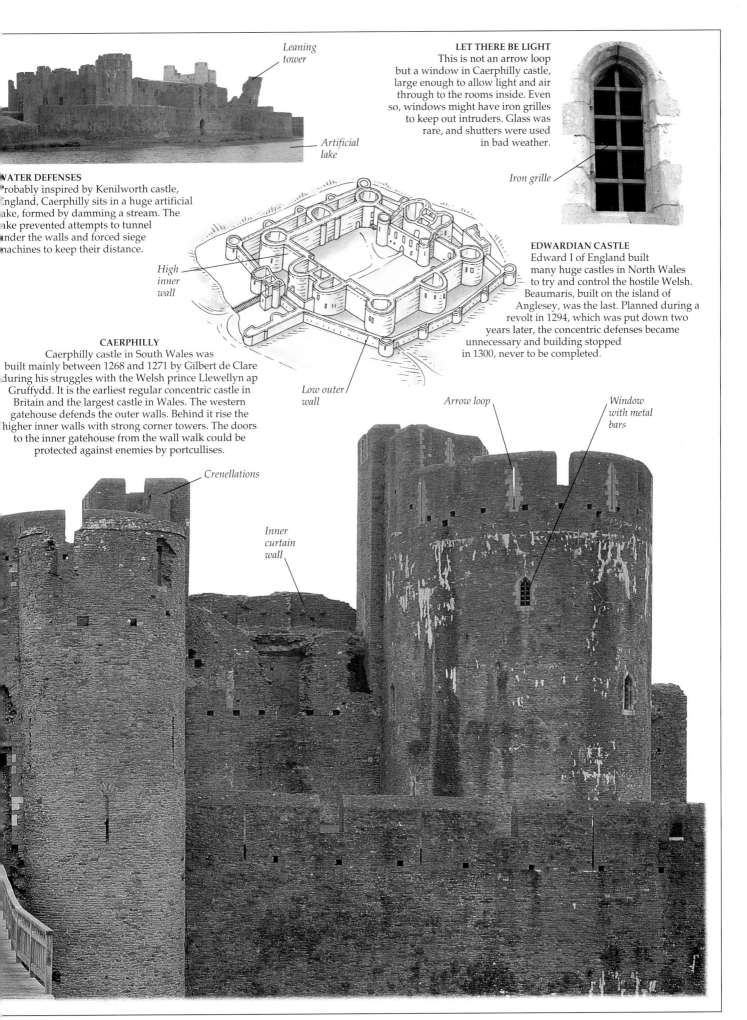

Leaning tower

Artificial lake

LET THERE BE LIGHT
This is not an arrow loop but a window in Caerphilly castle, large enough to allow light and air through to the rooms inside. Even so, windows might have iron grilles to keep out intruders. Glass was rare, and shutters were used in bad weather.

Iron grille

WATER DEFENSES
Probably inspired by Kenilworth castle, England, Caerphilly sits in a huge artificial lake, formed by damming a stream. The lake prevented attempts to tunnel under the walls and forced siege machines to keep their distance.

High inner wall

Low outer wall

EDWARDIAN CASTLE
Edward I of England built many huge castles in North Wales to try and control the hostile Welsh. Beaumaris, built on the island of Anglesey, was the last. Planned during a revolt in 1294, which was put down two years later, the concentric defenses became unnecessary and building stopped in 1300, never to be completed.

CAERPHILLY
Caerphilly castle in South Wales was built mainly between 1268 and 1271 by Gilbert de Clare during his struggles with the Welsh prince Llewellyn ap Gruffydd. It is the earliest regular concentric castle in Britain and the largest castle in Wales. The western gatehouse defends the outer walls. Behind it rise the higher inner walls with strong corner towers. The doors to the inner gatehouse from the wall walk could be protected against enemies by portcullises.

Arrow loop

Window with metal bars

Crenellations

Inner curtain wall

Castles on the Loire

MANY CASTLES were built along the Loire River in France. Doue-La-Fontaine, probably the oldest known keep, was one of the first. French castles developed during the reign of Philip Augustus (1180-1226) with powerful keeps, enclosures, round towers, and towers *en bec* (like a beak) on which the outward-facing side is drawn out like a ship's prow. Flying turrets jutted from walls without reaching the ground, and towers often had tall, conical roofs. In the 15th century, French castles became more luxurious.

Polychrome jug

Floor tiles

FRENCH TASTES
The 14th-century polychrome (many-colored) jug is in typical French style. The floor tiles are from Saumur castle and bear heraldic pictures. The fleur-de-lys was used in French royal arms and became the symbol of the French royal house. It therefore appeared in the coats of arms of a number of people related to the royal family.

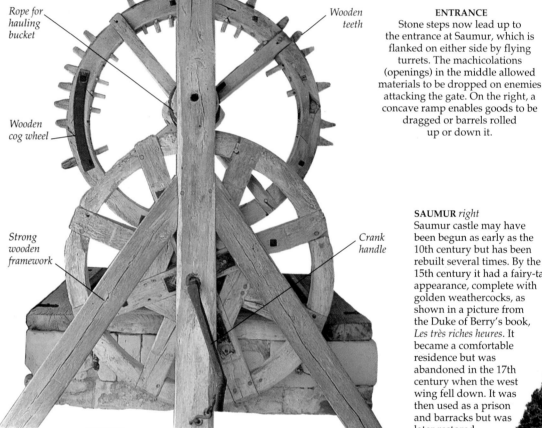

Rope for hauling bucket

Wooden teeth

Wooden cog wheel

Strong wooden framework

Crank handle

WINDER
At Saumur, water could be brought up from an underground well using these winding wheels. The wheels are made of wood and the teeth of one mesh with holes in the other.

ENTRANCE
Stone steps now lead up to the entrance at Saumur, which is flanked on either side by flying turrets. The machicolations (openings) in the middle allowed materials to be dropped on enemies attacking the gate. On the right, a concave ramp enables goods to be dragged or barrels rolled up or down it.

SAUMUR *right*
Saumur castle may have been begun as early as the 10th century but has been rebuilt several times. By the 15th century it had a fairy-tale appearance, complete with golden weathercocks, as shown in a picture from the Duke of Berry's book, *Les très riches heures*. It became a comfortable residence but was abandoned in the 17th century when the west wing fell down. It was then used as a prison and barracks but was later restored.

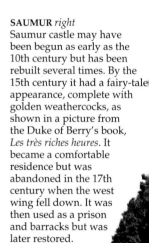

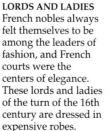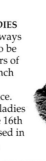

LORDS AND LADIES
French nobles always felt themselves to be among the leaders of fashion, and French courts were the centers of elegance. These lords and ladies of the turn of the 16th century are dressed in expensive robes.

THE VINEYARDS
The illustration of September from the Duke of Berry's *Les très riches heures*, written in about 1416, shows the grape harvest in the vineyard below the whitewashed walls of Saumur castle. The lower windows have iron grilles to stop people from getting in. The upper parts, although machicolated, have fantastic Gothic-style carved traceries (ornamental bars). The barbican (outer) gate has both a small and large lifting bridge. On its left are small jutting latrine blocks which drop waste into ditches. To their left is the tall chimney of the kitchen, isolated to guard against spreading fire.

Stair
tower

Well
house

WELL
The courtyard at Saumur has a well with a large underground water tank. This tank extends under the covered well house on the left, which contains the winding mechanism for lifting large buckets.

Corner
tower

Stair turret with
conical roof

Machicolations

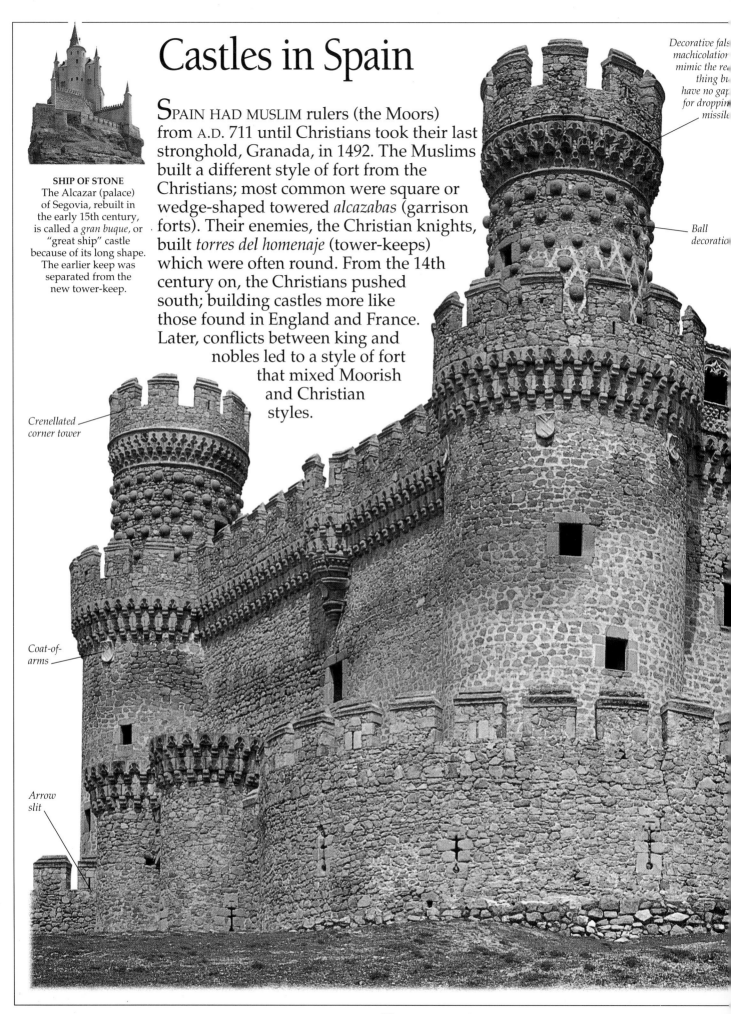

Castles in Spain

SPAIN HAD MUSLIM rulers (the Moors) from A.D. 711 until Christians took their last stronghold, Granada, in 1492. The Muslims built a different style of fort from the Christians; most common were square or wedge-shaped towered *alcazabas* (garrison forts). Their enemies, the Christian knights, built *torres del homenaje* (tower-keeps) which were often round. From the 14th century on, the Christians pushed south; building castles more like those found in England and France. Later, conflicts between king and nobles led to a style of fort that mixed Moorish and Christian styles.

SHIP OF STONE
The Alcazar (palace) of Segovia, rebuilt in the early 15th century, is called a *gran buque*, or "great ship" castle because of its long shape. The earlier keep was separated from the new tower-keep.

Decorative fals
machicolation
mimic the rea
thing bu
have no gap
for droppin
missile

Ball
decoratio

Crenellated
corner tower

Coat-of-
arms

Arrow
slit

22

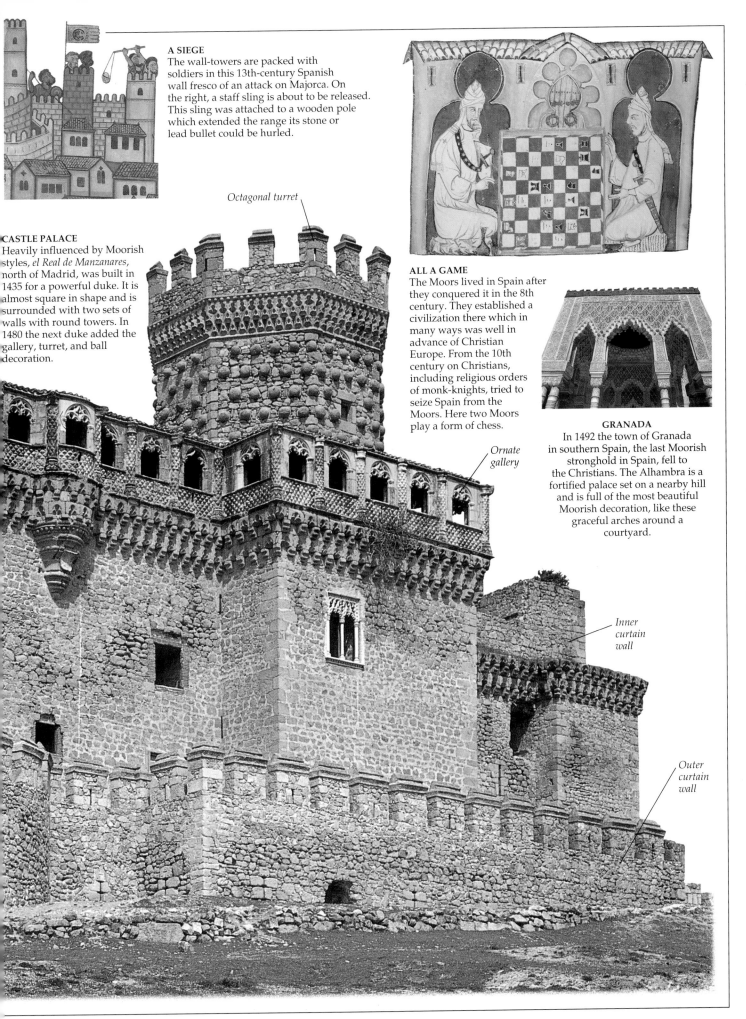

A SIEGE

The wall-towers are packed with soldiers in this 13th-century Spanish wall fresco of an attack on Majorca. On the right, a staff sling is about to be released. This sling was attached to a wooden pole which extended the range its stone or lead bullet could be hurled.

Octagonal turret

CASTLE PALACE

Heavily influenced by Moorish styles, *el Real de Manzanares*, north of Madrid, was built in 1435 for a powerful duke. It is almost square in shape and is surrounded with two sets of walls with round towers. In 1480 the next duke added the gallery, turret, and ball decoration.

ALL A GAME

The Moors lived in Spain after they conquered it in the 8th century. They established a civilization there which in many ways was well in advance of Christian Europe. From the 10th century on Christians, including religious orders of monk-knights, tried to seize Spain from the Moors. Here two Moors play a form of chess.

Ornate gallery

GRANADA

In 1492 the town of Granada in southern Spain, the last Moorish stronghold in Spain, fell to the Christians. The Alhambra is a fortified palace set on a nearby hill and is full of the most beautiful Moorish decoration, like these graceful arches around a courtyard.

Inner curtain wall

Outer curtain wall

23

Castles in Germany

IN WHAT IS NOW GERMANY, many princes and nobles lived in castles under the leadership of an emperor. As central control broke down in the 13th century, many lesser lords also built castles, some as bases for robbery. German castle design was often influenced by the land. Many castles took advantage of hills and mountains; others were built along the banks of the Rhine River. In flatter areas the *Wasserburg*, a type of castle protected by a wide moat, was seen. The Teutonic Order of monk-knights built brick castles like blockhouses (structures for defense), containing residential and religious areas set around a rectangular courtyard. Most large 11th- and 12th-century castles were later given a curtain wall with flanking towers.

POTTERY
This type of pottery is known as Rhenish ware because it was made in the Rhineland. It was often exported to other countries. These jugs would have been "thrown" on a potter's wheel and partly glazed to add color.

LONG OCCUPATION
Schloss Mespelbrunn at Spessart, Bavaria, began as a medieval castle and was rebuilt in the 16th century to suit the taste for more comfort. Because the castle sits in a huge moat, its builders could put large windows in the outer walls.

HILLTOP HOME
Cochem castle sits on a hill overlooking the Moselle River. It was probably begun in about 1020. The tall *Bergfried*, or tower, is typically German. The castle was used as a toll station, and there was a chain to bar the river.

Handle

Spout

Hollow body for water

LION JUG
The aquamanile was a type of metal or pottery jug that had a spout to pour water for washing hands at mealtimes. Different forms of aquamanile were made, including jugs in the shape of knights on horseback. This German copper-alloy lion has a man sitting astride its back, pulling its ears.

WAY IN
The entrance to the castle of Pfalzgrafenstein is guarded by a wooden portcullis sheathed in iron. Instead of moving up and down slots within the gate passage, the portcullis is set against the wall and slides through slots cut in stone brackets. Above the lifting chains are the curved arches of machicolations. On the right of the gate is an opening protected by a wooden shutter.

ISLAND CASTLE
The five-sided tower of the Pfalzgrafenstein was built as a toll-station on an island in the Rhine by King Ludwig I of Bavaria in 1327.

HOME COMFORTS
The latrine, or toilet, has a wooden seat to give added comfort.

THE ENCLOSURE
This view from the tower of the Pfalzgrafenstein shows the domestic buildings set against the inner side of the enclosure walls. A covered wooden gallery runs alongside these buildings. In the middle is one of the circular turrets which covers the angle where two walls meet.

A CASTLE RE-USED
The hexagonal enclosure of the Pfalzgrafenstein was added between about 1338 and 1342 to create a turret fortress, a type of castle typical of western Germany. Useful even after the end of the Middle Ages, it was strengthened further in 1607, when one end was given a protruding bastion.

Belfry on medieval tower

Gun ports

Window

Wooden hoarding for defence

Seventeenth-century bastion

The stonemasons

OF ALL MEDIEVAL CRAFTSMEN, skilled masons were the most highly paid and respected. It was they who built the great cathedrals and castles that still rise above many European towns and cities. Before they formed exclusive guilds in the 14th century, masons organized their trade from their lodges. These were the masons' headquarters on the building site where they worked in bad weather, ate their meals, and discussed trade secrets. Rules and working conditions were set out by the lodge leaders. Masons learned their craft on the site itself, often serving an apprenticeship of up to seven years. The most talented might go on to become master masons, with the responsibility for designing and overseeing the building of an entire cathedral.

"Stock" rests on top of the stone

Blade measures depth

SQUARED UP
The square was one of the mason's most important tools. It was used for making sure corners were straight.

SINKING SQUARE
Each stone had to be worked precisely to shape before being hoisted into position. The sinking square was used to measure the depth of holes or grooves and to check that the corners were square.

SCORING A CURVE
The mason had to mark out his stone to show him where to cut or carve. To mark a curved line parallel to the edge, he used a box trammel. Holding the wooden handle firmly against the edge, he dragged it along. The trammel point moved across the stone, scoring a line.

Sharp point scores the stone

PITCHER THIS
Every single stone in a cathedral would have taken about a day to cut and finish. Because it was heavy and expensive to transport, the stone was cut approximately to size at the quarry. At the building site, the mason's first job was to finish cutting the rough stone with a big curved saw. Then he used a hammer, a heavy, blunt chisel called a pitching tool, and a punch (right) to chip off the larger lumps and produce nearly straight edges.

Pitching tool for making clean breaks in rough stone

Well-worn chisel-head

Hammer-headed chisels

Punch for chipping off large bits of stone

HEAVY LUMP
The lump hammer was used for hitting hammer-headed chisels in the rough shaping work.

UNITED BY DIVIDERS
Dividers, or wing compasses, became the mason's special emblem. They were used mainly to measure a distance on a template, and then transfer the measurement to a piece of stone.

Medieval dividers

Template for the cross-section of the joint

Joint

Paper template for a piece of window tracery

Modern masons mark out a block with pencil lines

MARKING OUT
The mason selected a block of stone that had been trimmed square and smooth on which to mark out the template. He then scribed, or scratched, around the edges.

ACCORDING TO PLAN
The template, or pattern, for each stone was cut out of board, leather, or parchment and laid over the stone for the mason to copy.

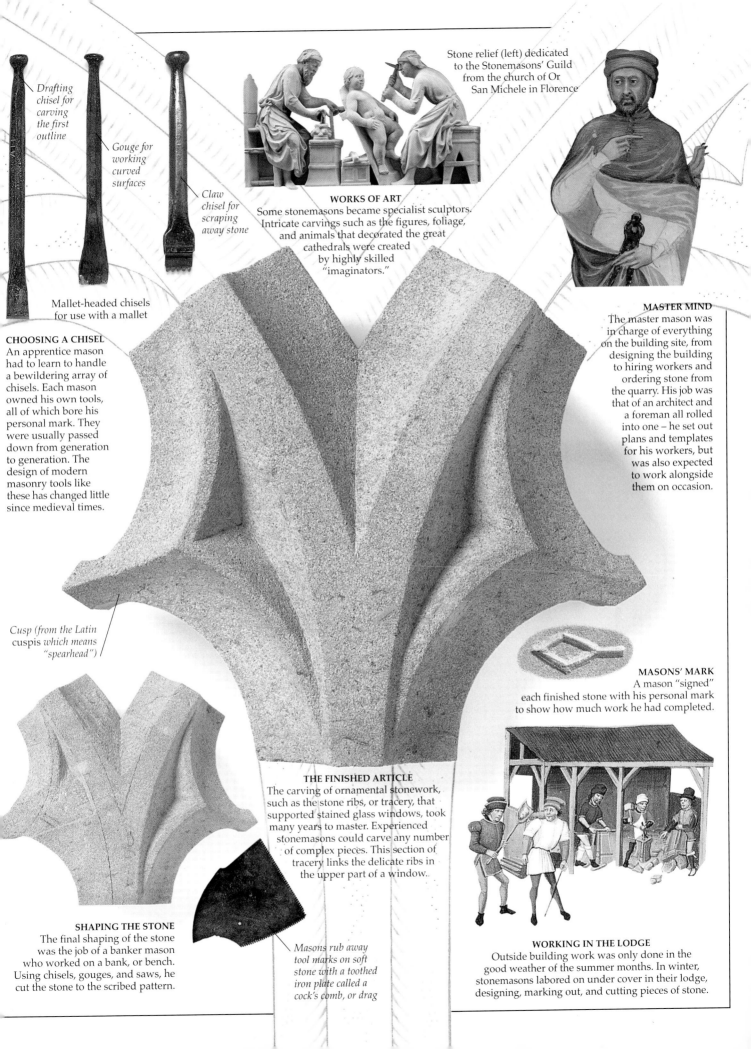

Drafting chisel for carving the first outline

Gouge for working curved surfaces

Claw chisel for scraping away stone

Mallet-headed chisels for use with a mallet

CHOOSING A CHISEL
An apprentice mason had to learn to handle a bewildering array of chisels. Each mason owned his own tools, all of which bore his personal mark. They were usually passed down from generation to generation. The design of modern masonry tools like these has changed little since medieval times.

WORKS OF ART
Some stonemasons became specialist sculptors. Intricate carvings such as the figures, foliage, and animals that decorated the great cathedrals were created by highly skilled "imaginators."

Stone relief (left) dedicated to the Stonemasons' Guild from the church of Or San Michele in Florence

MASTER MIND
The master mason was in charge of everything on the building site, from designing the building to hiring workers and ordering stone from the quarry. His job was that of an architect and a foreman all rolled into one – he set out plans and templates for his workers, but was also expected to work alongside them on occasion.

Cusp (from the Latin cuspis *which means "spearhead")*

MASONS' MARK
A mason "signed" each finished stone with his personal mark to show how much work he had completed.

THE FINISHED ARTICLE
The carving of ornamental stonework, such as the stone ribs, or tracery, that supported stained glass windows, took many years to master. Experienced stonemasons could carve any number of complex pieces. This section of tracery links the delicate ribs in the upper part of a window.

SHAPING THE STONE
The final shaping of the stone was the job of a banker mason who worked on a bank, or bench. Using chisels, gouges, and saws, he cut the stone to the scribed pattern.

Masons rub away tool marks on soft stone with a toothed iron plate called a cock's comb, or drag

WORKING IN THE LODGE
Outside building work was only done in the good weather of the summer months. In winter, stonemasons labored on under cover in their lodge, designing, marking out, and cutting pieces of stone.

The woodworkers

WOODEN CASTLES were far more common than those of stone before the 12th century. Professional woodworkers were needed to cut the timber for palisade fences and walkways, the gate tower, motte tower, bailey buildings, and sometimes facings (called revetments) covering the slope of the motte and the bailey ditch banks. When stone castles became popular, some of the defenses were still made of wood. In addition, large amounts of wooden scaffolding were needed as the building rose up. Courtyard buildings were often made of wood or built with a wooden frame. Even in stone buildings wood was used for roof and ceiling beams and floors. Inside, carpenters made doors, shutters, partitions, paneling, and furniture. During a siege they would make catapults and other machines (see pp. 84–85) to help defend the castle.

HOARDINGS
Removable wooden hoardings were supported on beams pushed into holes called putlog holes below the battlements.

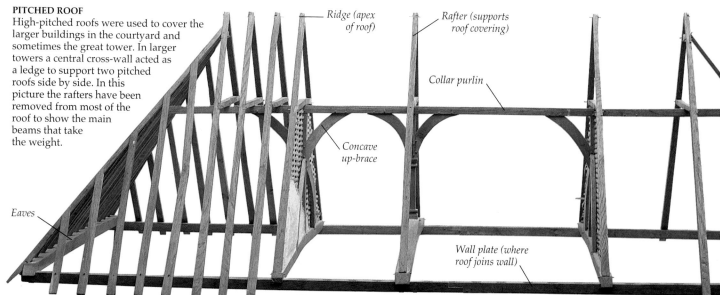

PITCHED ROOF
High-pitched roofs were used to cover the larger buildings in the courtyard and sometimes the great tower. In larger towers a central cross-wall acted as a ledge to support two pitched roofs side by side. In this picture the rafters have been removed from most of the roof to show the main beams that take the weight.

Ridge (apex of roof)

Rafter (supports roof covering)

Collar purlin

Concave up-brace

Eaves

Wall plate (where roof joins wall)

PLANE TO SEE
Beams or planks were planed, which gave them a smooth finish.

HOLD IT
Several methods were used to connect pieces of wood. Usually a joint was made by cutting the ends so that one piece fit snugly into or over the other. Wooden pegs were hammered through drilled holes to strengthen the bond.

WOODEN LEAVES
This door has two leaves, or panels. Main castle doors were made of massively thick planks, sometimes strengthened by iron bands. They were held shut by locks and wooden drawbars – beams which slid into holes in the wall to bar the door. Two-leaved doors might instead be secured by a pivoting bar attached to the door by a central pin.

SAW POINT
These workmen are cutting a large piece of wood with a two-handed saw. Sometimes a saw-pit was used, the lower-ranking man standing in the pit, where he was showered with shavings.

Auger

Hammer

TOOLS OF THE TRADE
The tools used by medieval carpenters were very similar to those of today. The auger was twisted around to bore holes; the handsaw cut small pieces of wood. The metal parts were made by a smith (pp. 30–31).

Handsaw

BAD WORKER
This early 14th-century tile from Tring, England, shows a master craftsman telling off a worker for cutting a beam too short. Workers of various professions were organized into guilds, with rules and standards of quality to be kept up.

CARPENTER
Skilled woodworkers were always in demand because of the large number of objects made from this material. Unlike today, large areas of countryside were covered in woodland and forest, and timber was carefully managed to make sure supplies were always at hand. Once a castle was built there was always need for a carpenter to repair or replace damaged items, or woodwork damaged by insects, fungi, or the damp.

Tie-beam

Awls

Billhook

Broad ax

Adze (for cutting slivers from the surface)

Chisel

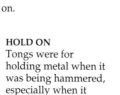

Metalwork

METALS OF ALL KINDS were used in castles. Iron was needed for a number of different everyday things, from horseshoes and harnesses to parts for siege machines, door hinges, tools, and hoops for barrels. Nails, both large and small, were used by the thousands for joining wood to construct palisades, wooden buildings, and parts of buildings such as roofs and doors. All these items had to be made by a metalworker (or smith) in the castle itself. The lord would frequently buy armor for himself and his knights from local merchants. A rich lord might even have some of his armor made abroad. But weapons and armor were in constant use. They were damaged in training and rivets would work loose. A castle armorer was needed for equipment repairs.

CLOSE WORK
If a seamstress needed a thimble to protect her finger, a metalworker had to make it. This one might have been bought from a market, a shop, or a traveling merchant.

STRIKING A POSE
The smiths in this 15th-century manuscript are busily hammering metal into shape over a solid iron anvil, their tools hanging behind them. Some anvils had a "beak" at one end, which was used to shape metal objects like horseshoes, but the anvil used by armorers was often a simple cube of iron. Most smiths' workshops were housed in a separate building to reduce the risk of the rest of the castle catching fire.

ARMED AND DANGEROUS
Armor and weapons like those of this 16th-century knight were often damaged in battle or tournament. An armorer who could do repairs, replace loose or broken rivets, and make pieces of mail and plate armor when needed was a valuable asset in a castle.

Cutting edge

A SNIP
Snips were for cutting sheets of metal to give a basic shape to work on.

HOLD ON
Tongs were for holding metal when it was being hammered, especially when it was red hot.

Handles

Metal tools

These medieval tools are little different from those used today. Armorers had extra tools, such as a huge pair of snips, set vertically with one end fixed to a block, to cut sheets of steel for making plate armour.

NIPPERS
The pincers could cut through wire. They have a swiveling fastener to hold them closed.

Swivel fastener

COPPER
A 14th-century smith shapes copper. Softer than other metals, copper was used for decorative work.

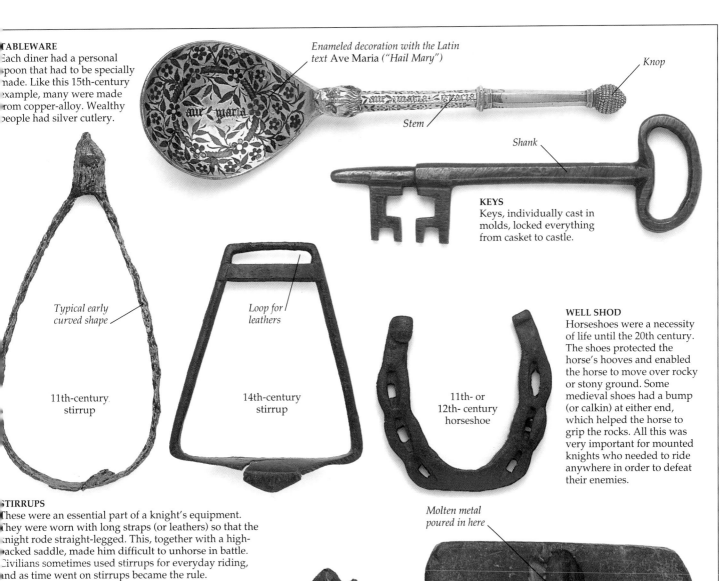

TABLEWARE
Each diner had a personal spoon that had to be specially made. Like this 15th-century example, many were made from copper-alloy. Wealthy people had silver cutlery.

Enameled decoration with the Latin text Ave Maria *("Hail Mary")*

Knop

Stem

Shank

KEYS
Keys, individually cast in molds, locked everything from casket to castle.

Typical early curved shape

11th-century stirrup

Loop for leathers

14th-century stirrup

11th- or 12th- century horseshoe

WELL SHOD
Horseshoes were a necessity of life until the 20th century. The shoes protected the horse's hooves and enabled the horse to move over rocky or stony ground. Some medieval shoes had a bump (or calkin) at either end, which helped the horse to grip the rocks. All this was very important for mounted knights who needed to ride anywhere in order to defeat their enemies.

STIRRUPS
These were an essential part of a knight's equipment. They were worn with long straps (or leathers) so that the knight rode straight-legged. This, together with a high-backed saddle, made him difficult to unhorse in battle. Civilians sometimes used stirrups for everyday riding, and as time went on stirrups became the rule.

Molten metal poured in here

MOLDED
Some items were made by melting metal and pouring it into a mold. This 15th-century figure is made from lead, which melts at a low temperature and was therefore easy to cast in this way. Lead was often used for making badges.

FORGE
This 19th-century picture of a forge shows that metalworkers were still using similar tools and techniques as their medieval counterparts..

Figure

Mold

Medieval society

TOP OF THE TREE
In this 14th-century picture, a French king presides over a gathering of his most important vassals, with the bishops on one side and barons on the other.

GOD'S DEPUTY
Medieval kings were seen as God's deputies on earth. A coronation was a magnificent religious ceremony; archbishops anointed the new king with holy oil as a sign of his status.

SOCIETY IN MUCH OF medieval Europe was organized into a "feudal" system, which was based on the allocation of land in return for services. The king gave fiefs, or grants of land, to his most important noblemen (barons and bishops), and in return, each noble promised to supply the king with soldiers in time of war. A noble pledged himself to be the king's vassal, or servant, at a special ceremony – kneeling before the king, he swore an oath of loyalty with the words "Sire, I become your man." The great nobles often divided their lands among lower lords, or knights, who in turn became their vassals. In this way, feudalism stretched from the top to the bottom of society. At the very bottom were the peasants who worked the land itself. They had few rights, little property – and no vassals.

TAXES NOT AXES
By about 1100, many vassals were unwilling to fight for their king. Instead, they were allowed to pay a sum of cash, called "scutage," or shield money, which could be used to hire soldiers. Scutage was one of the first regular money taxes levied by kings from their noblemen. A system of tax collectors (above) made sure that the full amounts were paid.

THE PEASANTS
The peasants were at the bottom of the feudal tree. They were the workers who farmed the land to provide food for everyone else. Most peasants worked for a lord who let them farm a piece of land for themselves in return for their labor (p. 44).

THE BARONS
Barons (p. 38) were the most powerful and wealthy noblemen, and received their fiefs directly from the king. When William of Normandy (p. 7) conquered England in 1066, he had about 120 barons. Each provided him with a possible army of over 5,000 men.

THE LORDS
Lords ruled over fiefs or manors (p. 40), renting out most of their land to the peasants who worked for them. They were also the warriors of medieval society. As trained knights, they were bound by oath to serve the great nobles who granted them their fiefs, and they could be called to battle at any time.

Bishop wears a miter (p. 37) as a sign of his status

King is mockingly portrayed with a cat on his head!

THE BISHOPS

Bishops often wielded as much power as the barons. They ruled over areas called dioceses (p. 37) and all the priests and monasteries within them. The regular collection of tithes (p. 47) and other taxes from their dioceses made many bishops extremely rich.

THE KING

Few kings had enough wealth to keep a standing army and depended on their barons to provide knights and soldiers. But kings had to work hard to keep their barons under control (p. 34). In many cases, especially in France and Germany, the great barons grew very powerful and governed their fiefs as independent states.

ROUGH JUSTICE

In the Middle Ages, ordinary people had few rights. Those who broke the law were tried in the court of their lord, who had almost complete power over them. Punishment for crimes was often harsh – a convicted criminal might be dragged behind a horse, whipped, locked in the stocks, or hanged, depending on the nature of his or her crime. But being at the top of the feudal system did not always ensure better treatment. Lords and barons sometimes had to pay their king large sums of money to get a fair trial. The medieval Church operated its own justice system with its own laws (the canon laws) and courts (p. 37) that were outside the jurisdiction of the king.

The royal court

Love-heart decorated with tears

THE ROYAL COURT was the center and the showpiece of the kingdom. Here a monarch demonstrated his power with grand ceremonies and banquets, collected taxes, settled disputes, and made laws. It was particularly important to maintain control over the powerful barons. Henry II of England (1133–1189) held special court sessions to sort out arguments over land-holding, and Louis IX of France (1214–1270) insisted on listening to cases in person. Other monarchs amazed their subjects and visitors alike with the magnificence of their courts. Most astounding of all were the Sicilian castles of the Holy Roman Emperor (p. 32) Frederick II (1194–1250), which had golden floors, exotic animals, beautiful gardens, and dancing girls.

THE RIGHT TO RULE
Most medieval kings believed they had absolute power over their subjects, given to them by God. This sometimes led them to arrogant gestures – and disaster. Richard II of England (1367–1400) once sat for hours on his throne, glancing around. He merely wanted to watch his courtiers kneel when he looked at them. By 1399, Richard's despotic ways had made him so unpopular that he was deposed from his throne.

Lances measure about 13 ft (4 m)

LYRICS OF LOVE
Every court had its minstrels, who sang songs about love and brave deeds, accompanying themselves on the harp or the lute (p. 110). The greatest love songs were written by the troubadours, who flourished in southern France in the 12th century. Each troubadour wrote in praise of his idealized lady love.

LANCE A LOT
To rebel against the king was equivalent to defying God, but if a king was weak or poor, his powerful barons could be troublesome (pp. 38 – 39). Monarchs were eager to lure their noblemen to court, where they could keep an eye on them. One great attraction was the joust, a contest of fighting skills. Here, two armored knights canter toward each other, their lances held before them. The object was to hit your opponent on the head or chest and knock him off his horse.

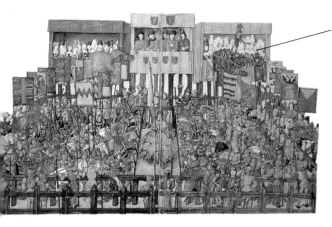

Court ladies watch the tournament from the stand

Glittering shield may have been presented as a tournament prize

WAR GAMES
Pomp and ceremony were important parts of court life. The tourney, or mock battle, was a popular and spectacular way of amusing the court in the 11th century. While the king, queen, and courtiers looked on, large parties of knights charged at each other. If they were unhorsed, they went on fighting on foot. Tourneys were bloody and dangerous: during one fight at Cologne, more than 60 knights were killed.

"Tables" counter for playing a game similar to backgammon

IDLE PASTIMES
The lords and ladies of the court whiled away idle hours with indoor games such as backgammon, chess, and dice. Playing cards became popular in the 13th century.

OFFICIAL BUSINESS
The king made his wishes known through writs. His scribe's office produced hundreds of documents each year granting lands, and permission to raise armies, appoint officials, and order the payment of taxes. This writ, dated 1291, is a grant of game rights from Edward I of England (1239–1307) to one of his barons, Roger de Pilkington.

The royal seal makes the document official

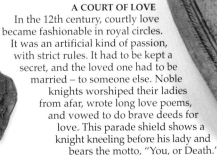

A COURT OF LOVE
In the 12th century, courtly love became fashionable in royal circles. It was an artificial kind of passion, with strict rules. It had to be kept a secret, and the loved one had to be married – to someone else. Noble knights worshiped their ladies from afar, wrote long love poems, and vowed to do brave deeds for love. This parade shield shows a knight kneeling before his lady and bears the motto, "You, or Death."

15th-century Flemish shield

The Church

THE CATHOLIC CHURCH was at the center of the medieval world. Unlike today, it was the only church in Europe, and all Christians belonged to it. With its own laws, lands, and taxes, the Church was a powerful institution. It governed almost every aspect of people's lives, from the practical to the spiritual. Most men and women, rich and poor, were baptized and married in church and attended mass every Sunday of their lives. When they died, their priest read them the last rites, and they were buried on church ground. For many, life on Earth was hard and short, but the Church said that if they followed the teachings of Christ, they would be rewarded in heaven. This idea gave the Church great power over people's hearts and minds.

LEADERS OF MEN
Archbishops were powerful men who sat on the king's council and played a leading role in government.

Censer is suspended on gilded chains

BIRD OF BLESSING
Suspended above the altar, this golden dove symbolized the Holy Spirit during the Eucharist – the Catholic ceremony where bread and wine are blessed and eaten to commemorate the sacrifice of Christ.

CHURCH TREASURES
By the 14th century, the Church had grown hugely wealthy. Money poured in from rents, tithes (p. 47), and the sale of indulgences (pardons for sins). Larger churches could afford to buy expensive sacramental vessels like this beautiful 14th-century silver chalice.

PARISH PRACTICES
The life of a parish priest was often a hard one. Many were poor men who lacked any serious education. Most of a priest's income came from fees charged for baptisms (above), marriages, and burial services. He also had his own land in the village, called the glebe, where he grew his own food. Apart from preaching, a village priest tended to the sick and poor, and the better-educated taught Latin and Bible stories to local boys.

Burning incense is placed inside the censer

SWINGING CENSERS
During mass, priests swung censers full of burning incense to purify the air. People believed that by attending mass regularly, they would be rewarded by God – and the more masses, the greater the reward. The wealthy could pay to have the "Trental," or 30 masses, said for them.

VISIONS OF HELL
The Church taught that when a person died, the good and bad deeds of their life were literally weighed in the balance by God. Their soul was either carried to heaven by angels or dragged off to hell by demons. Hell was a real and terrifying place for people in medieval times, and its torments were pictured in vivid detail in numerous paintings.

Carved wooden angels from a medieval church nave, or central hall

Angel holds a tiny church

Angel holds a gilded casket

CONDEMNED TO THE FLAMES
Few people challenged the authority of the Church, but those who did were severely punished. People who disagreed with the Church's teachings were called heretics. They faced being brought to trial in a church court and, under its special laws, could be condemned to be whipped or burned at the stake. The Cathar sect of southern France rejected the beliefs of the Catholic Church with their claims that everything on Earth was created by the devil. In 1208, the Pope ordered a crusade against these heretics. Over the next 26 years, thousands of Cathars were tortured and burned in huge bonfires until they had been completely wiped out.

Angel swings a golden censer

BISHOP'S MITER
Bishops were the local leaders of the Church. From their great cathedrals, they ruled over groups of parishes called dioceses. They usually came from noble families and were involved in affairs of state as well as those of the Church. Some were pious and learned men, but others were not – one 13th-century Italian bishop admitted that he did not believe in Christianity, and had only taken the office "because of its riches and honors."

Picture shows the coronation of the Virgin by Christ

14th-century bishop's miter, or hat

VICAR OF CHRIST
The Pope was head of the whole Church and represented God on Earth. This massive gilt ring belonged to Pope Eugenius IV, who ruled from 1431 to 1437.

The great barons

EVERY NOBLEMAN was a vassal (p. 32) who had promised to serve his king. But many nobles grew so powerful that kings could not control them. By the 12th century, the strongest barons ruled what were really tiny, self-contained states with their own laws. The finery of their castle-courts often rivaled that of the king's, and many kept permanent armies at their beck and call. One French baron, the Sire de Coucy, had a bodyguard of 50 knights, each with ten followers. These small private armies sometimes rode out to plunder their neighbors in savage and pitiless raids. They posed a serious threat to the king if he did not keep his barons happy.

PARLIAMENTARY PIONEER
The English king usually governed through a Great Council of barons and churchmen. But Simon de Montfort (c. 1208–1265) wanted to limit the powers of Henry III (1207–1272). He led a rebellion in 1264, took the king prisoner, and summoned the first "parliament." This was made up of the old Council, plus two representatives from each county and town

HIT MEN
Barons sometimes hired mercenary troops to do their fighting for them. These were bands of up to 3,000 soldiers of all nationalities – deserters from the Crusades, outlaws, and exiled knights.

VLAD DRACUL
Most infamous of all barons was the ghoulish Vlad Tepes of Romania (c. 1430–1476). According to legend, he put thousands of people to death by impaling them on stakes. He was nicknamed "Dracula," or "Dragon's son."

RALLY ROUND THE FLAG
Every nobleman had a banner such as this showing his own colors and emblems. Such flags were important rallying points for soldiers and knights on the battlefield.

THE BOAST OF HERALDRY
When knights rode into battle, their faces were hidden behind armor. So they identified themselves by carrying a coat of arms, or device, on their shield. By the 13th century, these devices were used not just by warriors, but by powerful baronial families.

Composite 15th-century flag

WARLORD

Charging full tilt at a band of helpless civilians, a fully armored knight, his face hidden behind a great helmet, was a chilling sight. Describing an attack by the men of a great baron on the town of Durham, England, in 1143, a monk recounted: "All that came in their way was destroyed; men were hung from the walls of their own houses; others they plunged into the bed of the river; everywhere throughout the town there were groans and all kinds of deaths."

14th-century visored "basinet"

THE GREAT CHARTER

In June 1215, the English barons forced King John (1167–1216) to sign the Magna Carta (Great Charter). This document limited the king's rights to tax the barons and to punish any man without a proper trial. But the Magna Carta did not recommend equal rights for all – ordinary people were scarcely mentioned. However, it was a crucial moment, the first time an English king had come under the control of the law.

King John's Great Seal

Wheel pommel

Italian war hammer, late 15th century

German battle ax, late 15th century

Single-handed French sword, 14th century

Fortified gatehouse

MORTAL COMBAT

The baron sat as judge in his own law court. If he could not reach a clear decision, he might allow a trial by combat. Accused and accuser would put on armor and fight each other with sword and ax – whoever won the battle, won the case. Most people preferred to hire champions to fight for them. But this was not a popular line of work. The loser might be suspected of surrendering on purpose, and have his hand chopped off as a punishment!

Double-edged blade with numerous battle scars

KEEP OUT!

Dotted around the medieval countryside, castles were impressive military strongholds. By the 12th century, many had massive towers of stone surrounded by high walls up to 33 ft (10 m) thick. They were so well fortified that an invading army could not capture them by a direct attack, but had to settle for a long siege. One of the most massive was at Carcassonne in France (above), where the castle walls, with their 54 towers, enclosed the entire town.

Running a manor

Most country people lived on a manor, which consisted of a village, the lord's house or castle, a church, and the surrounding farmland. The lord of the manor governed the community and appointed officials who made sure that the villagers carried out their duties. These involved farming the demesne, or lord's land, and paying rents in the form of produce. The lord also acted as a judge in the manor court and had the power to fine those who broke the law. Since manors were often isolated, the villagers had to produce everything they needed themselves. Few goods, except salt for curing meat and iron for tools, came from outside. The only visitors were peddlers, pilgrims, or soldiers, and few people ever traveled far from their own village.

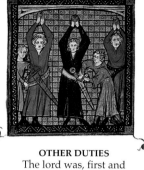

OTHER DUTIES
The lord was, first and foremost, a knight (p. 32) who provided arms for the king whenever he needed them. These knights are receiving their swords.

THE STEWARD
The lord left the daily running of his manor to a number of officials. The most important was the steward, who organized farmwork, kept accounts of the estate's money, and presided at the manor court if his master was away. Stewards were well-paid, powerful figures in the district.

Medieval watering pot

THE LORD AND LADY
The lord and lady of the manor had to oversee the running of the estate and their household, but they also had plenty of free time to pursue leisure activities. This French tapestry shows two angels holding a canopy over the heads of a noble and his lady, perhaps symbolizing their charmed lives!

THE MANOR HOUSE
The lord and his family lived in a large house that was often built of stone. It was surrounded by gardens and stables, and was protected by a high wall and sometimes by a moat. Apart from church activities, the manor house was the center of community life – its great hall served as the manor court and as the venue for special village feasts, such as those given after the harvest and at Christmastime

Favorite hawks were carried everywhere, even into church!

Peak keeps the sun out of the eyes and, when reversed, allows rainwater to run off

Felt hat

Brown doublet, or jacket

HAPPY HUNTING
Lords and ladies spent much of their time hunting, which was considered a noble pursuit. Many kept hawks to fly after rabbits or doves, and packs of hounds to chase deer or wild boar in their private woodlands.

THE BAILIFF
Next in importance to the steward was the bailiff. He was usually a peasant, which can be seen from his clothes – they were made from better material than those of a farm laborer, but were basically the same style. However, the bailiff was not a serf (p. 44), but a freeholder who owned his own land. He was in charge of giving jobs to the peasants, looking after the demesne's cattle, and taking care of repairs to buildings and tools, for which he hired skilled craftsmen such as carpenters and smiths.

GOING TO THE MILL
In most communities, there was only one watermill, which was owned by the lord. All other mills were often outlawed, so that the villagers were forced to use his mill for grinding their grain into flour. As payment, the lord kept some of their grain. Villagers might also have to bake their bread in the lord's oven and use his wine press for their grapes, for which they paid similar fees.

Woolen, linen-lined jacket with pewter buttons

Jacket was longer than that of a laborer

THE REEVE
The reeve was the bailiff's right-hand man. He was a peasant, chosen by the other villagers. Carrying a white stick as a badge of office, the reeve supervised work on the lord's demesne, checking that everyone began on time, and ensuring that none of the produce was stolen.

Stirrups pulled the hose closer to the leg for a fashionably slender look

Leather boots

The medieval soldier

Peace was rare in medieval times, especially in Europe. The Crusades against the Muslim Turks lasted for three centuries, and the Hundred Years' War between England and France dragged on from 1337 to 1453. Even when there were no major campaigns, barons and brigands raided their neighbors. In the early Middle Ages, the armored knight ruled the battlefield. He scorned the foot soldiers, who were mostly a rabble of poor, terrified, and untrained peasants, pressed into battle by their lords. But by the 15th century, knights were fast going out of fashion and ordinary soldiers became much more important. Lords began employing professional warriors, who were well-paid, skilled, and used to obeying orders. Many worked as mercenary soldiers, hiring themselves out to the highest bidder.

THE CRUSADES
In 1095, the Pope called for a holy war against the Muslim Turks who controlled the Christian Holy Land of Palestine. A European army set out on the First Crusade and managed to recapture the holy city of Jerusalem but the Turks soon advanced again. In all, there were eight crusades between 1147 and 1270, all of them failures. This 15th-century painting shows crusaders arriving at Damietta in Egypt.

"Glaive," a form of pole-weapon used for stabbing or knocking the enemy aside; it was safer to keep opponents at arm's length

Wooden drinking bowl for ale

Food bowl and spoon

ARCH ENEMY
Archers played a key role in the decline of the knight in the 15th century. Fired at the enemy from a safe distance, a deadly hail of arrows killed both men and horses. Without their horses, heavily armored knights were easy prey for foot soldiers.

Canvas kit bag

Cloth-charcoal, or tinder

Steel

Flint

Flint, steel, and tinder for lighting campfires

Chain splints keep swords from slicing through the arm

Sheepskin mitten worn inside

Mitten gauntlet protects the hand and wrist

Leather boots generally lasted about three months

FOOTSORE AND HUNGRY
Life on the march could be very hard. A foot soldier would have to walk at least 6 miles (10 km) a day, and occasionally three times as far. His food bowl was often empty, and a large army soon consumed everything edible in the surrounding countryside. Starving French soldiers in the First Crusade of 1097 were told to feed on their enemies: "Are there not corpses of Turks in plenty? Cooked and salted they will be good to eat!"

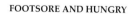

Peak protects the neck

Visor limited vision, so it was lowered only during fierce fighting

"Sallet" helmet

Military "bollock" dagger

Eating knife

HANDSOME RANSOM
A captured enemy could be a valuable acquisition. Important prisoners were often held to ransom for large sums of money. When King Richard I (1157–1199) of England was captured in 1194, his country had to pay 150,000 marks – a huge sum in those days.

BELT-BAG
A soldier had to carry his personal belongings with him wherever he went, so luggage was kept to a minimum. Slung from his belt, this leather purse probably contained money, dice for gambling, needles and thread, and a kerchief.

HAND-TO-HAND FIGHTING
With a sword in his right hand and a buckler in his left, a soldier was a dangerous enemy. The buckler was not only used to deflect blows, but also to hit an opponent in the face, before jabbing or slashing with the sword. However, the soldier did most of his fighting with a glaive, and relied on his sword as a last resort. There were no rules of combat in medieval warfare, and most battles were terrifying free-for-alls.

Gauntlet limits wrist movement

Small fist-shield, or buckler, for punching

I'M ALL RIGHT, JACK
This military outfit would have been worn by a professional foot soldier in the late 15th century. Some of his gear would have been issued to him, and the rest was probably stolen or looted. Most soldiers at this time wore much less armor than the knights of old. A padded tunic, called a jack, with iron gauntlets and arm splints, gave good protection against sword cuts and even flying arrows.

Thin leather belt

Quilted "jack" made from multi-layered canvas

Close-fitting canvas doublet

Single-handed sword for hand-to-hand combat

A peasant's life

Statue of a French peasant, c. 1500

ACCORDING TO THE LAW, medieval peasants did not belong to themselves. Everything, including their land, their animals, their homes, their clothes, and even their food, belonged to the lord of the manor (p. 40). Known as serfs or villeins, peasants were bound to work for their lord, who allowed them to farm their own piece of land in return. Their lives were ones of almost constant toil. Most struggled to produce enough food to feed their families as well as to fulfill their duties to the lord. Forbidden from leaving the manor without permission, the only way for a peasant to gain freedom was by saving enough money to buy a plot of land, or by marrying a free person.

Simple spoons can be cut from horn

Shepherd's horn pipe

DAILY GRIND
Peasants worked hard every day except Sundays and holy days, in blazing sun, rain, or snow. Combined with a poor diet, it isn't surprising that the average European peasant in 1300 lived no longer than 25 years.

Tired peasant wipes the sweat from his brow

DO IT YOURSELF
Peasants made some of their own tools and utensils, although skilled craftsmen produced their pottery, leatherwork, and iron. Besides wood and leather, the most important material was horn from cattle or sheep. Light and strong, it did not absorb flavors like wood and did not require great energy to shape. Horn spoons were easy to clean, according to one writer: "With a little licking they will always be kept as clean as a die."

THE PEASANTS' REVOLT
After the Black Death, there was a shortage of labor in 14th-century Europe. The peasants had to work harder than ever, and in England they also had to pay an extra tax. In 1381, the English peasants rose in rebellion. Led by Wat Tyler, they marched on London, where they murdered the archbishop. When they met the king, Richard II (1367–1400), he agreed to end the new tax, but Wat Tyler was killed in a quarrel. The peasant mob swiftly disbanded and went home. The French Jacquerie revolt of 1358 ended much more bloodily when armored knights slaughtered several thousand rebels.

Straw hat to protect
the head on hot days

Cheap pewter
badge for
good luck

Felt hat decorated
with a cockerel
feather and a "fleur-
de-lis" badge

Brown woolen jacket
lined with linen

Blue woolen doublet
fastened with "points"

Linen shirt

Linen underpants,
or braes

Leather flask, or
costrel, for carrying
ale into the fields

Peasants working
with their hose
rolled up

Woolen "split"
hose can be rolled
down for working

Leather working boots

PEASANT COTTAGE

Most peasants lived in simple homes like this
reconstructed 13th-century cottage. The walls
are made from local flint, but they were more
often made from wattle and daub – woven strips
of wood covered with a mixture of dung, straw,
and clay. Inside, the floor was bare, trampled
earth. Most cottages had only one or two rooms,
which contained basic furniture such as a trestle
table and bench, a chest for clothes, and straw
mattresses to sleep on. There was a stone hearth
in the center of the main room, but no chimney,
so it must have been very dark and smoky.

PLAIN CLOTHES

These are the kind of clothes that
would have been worn by a peasant
in the 1440s. Clothes, like tools, were
mostly homemade from local materials.
Peasant women spent much of their time
spinning wool into coarse thread, which
was then woven into cloth and made into
garments. Sheepskin cloaks were worn in
winter to keep out the cold and rain, and
wooden pattens (p. 49) could be put on
over leather boots in muddy conditions.
Although outer clothes were never
washed, linen underwear was
laundered regularly. People's
clothes generally smelled of
wood smoke, which had
a deodorizing effect!

Tied to the soil

IN MEDIEVAL EUROPE, more than 90 percent of the population lived and worked on the land. Farming was a full-time job, since methods were ancient and not very efficient. The crop-growing areas around a village were usually divided into three big fields. Peasants were allotted some land in each so that good and bad soil was shared out equally. They hoed and harvested their own strips, or plots, but worked together on big jobs such as plowing and hay-making. A failed harvest could mean starvation for the whole village.

Wooden pitchfork for lifting hay and wheat sheaves

HARVEST-TIME
In late summer, women and children worked alongside the men to bring in the harvest. They cut the wheat with sickles, grasping each clump firmly so that the grains wouldn't shake loose. The wheat was then tied in sheaves, or bundles, set in stooks, or shocks, in the field to ripen, loaded onto a cart, and taken to the barn. Once the harvest was in, the wheat was threshed – beaten with a flail, or hinged stick, to loosen the grains from the ears.

SOWING THE SEED
In the "three-field system," two fields were sown with crops in one year while the third was left fallow, or empty, so it could recover its strength. One field was sown with wheat in winter, and the next spring, the second was sown with rye, barley, or oats. Seeds were broadcast, or scattered, by hand.

Man knocking acorns out of an oak tree for his pigs

Seeds fell in the plowed furrows, but many were lost to hungry birds

Farmer broadcasts the seeds in a sweeping arc

Basket of seeds called a seedlip

AUTUMN ACORNS
Every autumn, the lord of the manor allowed his serfs to run their pigs in his private woods, where they could feed on acorns and beechnuts. Sheep, geese, and goats grazed on common wasteland at the edge of the village. Even so, most animals were thin and wiry.

Shafts for pulling the cart

Hungry pig

Peasants working together at harvest-time

MANUAL LABOR
With no machines, all farm work was done by hand using simple tools like these. Most jobs involved back-breaking labor, from breaking clods (lumps of soil) to hoeing young crops.

Billhook for maintaining hedges

Sickle for harvesting crops

SHEAR PROFIT
Sheep shearing was the most important spring job in hilly regions of medieval Europe. Wool fetched high prices, and its trade became one of the richest industries of the Middle Ages.

TITHE BARN
This huge 13th-century barn was used to store tithes. Villagers had to give the local priest a tithe, or tenth, of everything they produced, from crops and firewood to eggs and flour. Tithes made some churches very wealthy – and very unpopular.

Threshed wheat stalks, or straw

Rear gate is tied to keep the straw from falling out

Rim of wooden wheel is clad with six iron strakes for extra strength

CARTED OFF
Medieval peasants would have transported their wheat, straw, and hay in carts like this. Straw (the leftover stalks from the harvest) was used for numerous purposes, from thatching roofs to making mattresses. Hay was another important crop. Along with wheat straw and dried beans, it provided the only winter feed for farm animals. Even then, there was rarely enough for all, and most cattle, pigs, and goats had to be killed in late autumn. Every peasant had a share in the village's hay meadow, and hay-making was a communal task.

Large wheels allow the cart to ride over big bumps and ruts

Medieval women

"IT IS CLEAR," wrote a French priest in 1386, "that man is much nobler than woman, and of greater virtue." The medieval Church looked on women as inferior to men and taught that they should be meek and obedient to their fathers and husbands. But the real lives of women in the Middle Ages were rather different. Not all of them stayed quietly at home; most had to work for a living. Peasant women toiled alongside their husbands in the fields as well as having to feed and clothe their families. The wives and daughters of craftsmen were often employed in the workshop and frequently operated as tradeswomen in their own right. Wealthy ladies organized large households and sometimes ran their husbands' affairs. However, only a few powerful abbesses, noblewomen, and queens had any influence on national events.

KEEP IT COVERED
Although young single women often wore their hair loose, married women were expected to keep their hair covered in a linen "wimple" as a sign of modesty.

THE MAID OF ORLEANS
St. Joan (1412–1431) was a French peasant's daughter who, at the age of 13, heard voices telling her to drive the invading English army out of France. Dressed in armor, she led the French troops to a great victory at the besieged town of Orleans. However, Joan was later betrayed and sold to the English, who burned her as a witch.

GET THEE TO A NUNNERY
Many unmarried gentlewomen entered convents and nunneries, where they lived lives similar to those of monks (pp. 98 – 101). Nunneries offered women the opportunity to lead a devout life and also to obtain an education and take on responsibilities denied them in the outside world. As local landowners and employers, many abbesses were important figures in the community (above).

HOLDING THE FORT
This noblewoman has collapsed on hearing of her husband's death. Many women took on the responsibility of running large estates when their husbands died in battle or were away at court or on a crusade (p. 42). They settled local disputes, managed the farms, and handled finances. Some women even fought battles, defending their castles when they were under siege.

WOMEN OF WEALTH
Landowners, male or female, were powerful figures in medieval society, and an unmarried woman of property had equal legal rights with men. She could make a will, and sign documents with her own seal – this 13th-century seal belonged to a French noblewoman called Elizabeth of Sevorc. However, when a woman married, she forfeited her land and rights to her husband. On his death she was entitled to a third of his land with which to support herself.

48

SPINSTERS
Spinning was done almost entirely by women using hand-held spindles like this one (the spinning wheel was introduced from India in the 13th century). Many single women earned a living in this way, hence the term "spinster" for an unmarried woman.

Wool twists into thread as the spindle twirls

WRAP–UP
Most women covered their hair with white linen head-wraps, but the wealthy wore gold nets over their coiled braids. The well-known pointed hat called the hennin was only popular for a short time in the late 15th century.

Linen head-wrap keeps hair clean as well as hidden

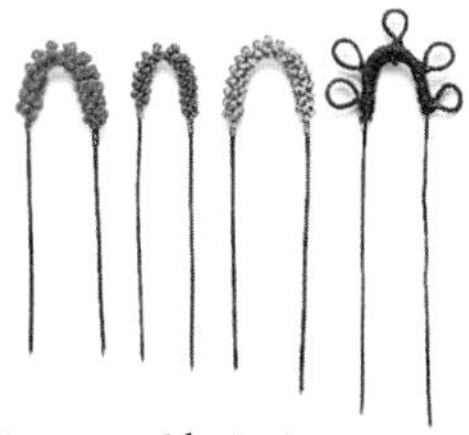

Decorated hairpins

Linen shift

Prayer beads

Pin-on sleeves worn on Sundays and special occasions

AN EARLY FEMINIST
Christine de Pisan (1364–1429) was one of the few medieval women to earn a living by writing. She wrote poetry and books protesting the way women were both glorified and insulted by male authors.

THE TOWNSWOMAN
A middle-class townswoman might have worn these clothes in the 15th century. In the towns, women worked in a variety of occupations. They might be shopkeepers, spinners, bakers, or "alewives," who brewed ale. Both married and unmarried women worked for a living. Because they were paid less than men, women often had two or more jobs.

Woolen "kirtle" fits close around the upper body

Leather purse serves as a pocket

Leather garters hold up stockings

Woolen over-the-knee stockings

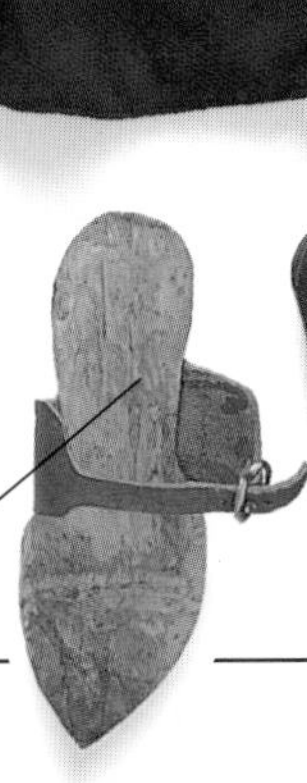

Wooden "pattens" worn over shoes when muddy

Buckled leather shoes with thin soles

The great hall

THE HALL WAS the main room in the castle. It was used for eating, sleeping, and carrying out business. The day in the hall began early with breakfast, which consisted of bread soaked in ale or watered wine, eaten after Mass. The main meal, where formality and good manners were expected, was taken at about ten or eleven in the morning. In the evening there were various suppers, which often ended in overeating and drunkenness. Servants with pitcher, basin, and napkin poured water over the hands of important guests before and after meals; other people washed at basins near the doors. Later the trestles (table supports) were removed to make room for entertainment and eventually palliasses (straw mattresses) for sleeping. Only rich people had beds. In the 13th century the lord began to distance himself from the larger household; extra rooms were built for him and his close family.

12th-century copper-alloy hanging lamp

Holder for candle

Modern drip-catcher

HEARTH AND HOME
Early halls had a fireplace in the middle of the room but these were later abandoned in favor of wall fireplaces, which had the advantage of a flue to carry away the smoke. The lord's table was often near the fire for warmth; it was usually situated at one end so the lord could survey the hall. Often on a raised platform, the lord's table might be the only one with fixed legs and a tablecloth.

FLOORED!
A 13th-century tile illustrates the legend of Tristan. The floors of royal palaces, rich halls, and abbeys were decorated with many tiles like this. Carpets were sometimes imported as luxuries from the East, but they were usually hung on the walls, like tapestries.

Silver bird holds shield with heraldic arms of the count of Flanders

Gilded mount

Maple-wood cover

Bowl made from very finely cut maple wood

Animal decoration

Decorative enameled design

CANDLESTICK
Animals and plants decorate this late 12th-century copper-alloy German candlestick. Candles were made from animal fats. Oil lamps were also used.

YOUR HEALTH!
Covered wooden bowls were sometimes used for drinking toasts. They were called mazers, an old word for maple, the wood used to make the bowls. This 15th-century Flemish bowl has a gilded silver foot. It probably belonged to Louis de Male, Count of Flanders. Another precious vessel in the great hall was the salt cellar. This was placed in front of the principal guest at mealtimes; smaller "salts" were placed on other tables. Lesser folk sat "below the salt."

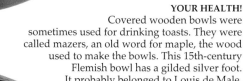

ROYAL HALL
Steps from the hall at Loches, France, led out to the battlements, marked by the round tower. Often the curtain wall formed one side of the hall. This saved money on building but meant that no large windows could be set into this side of the hall. Early halls had been made of timber, but stone became increasingly common. Because of the smell and risk of fire, the lord usually built his hall well away from the kitchen.

FORMAL MEALS
These took place in the great hall. Sometimes there was a lesser hall where the castle constable conducted business.

STEEP ROOF
The castle at Loches on the Loire River in France has a keep of the 11th and 12th centuries with many later additions. The royal hall with its stepped gable is associated with the 15th-century king Charles VII, whose mistress Agnes Sorel lived at Loches and is buried there.

Battlements of great hall

Conical, slate-covered roof

Door to tower and outer courtyard

Circular tower overlooks battlements, to give a good view of the surrounding area

Large upper windows of great hall

51

continued on next page

High table, low table

Dinner was the grandest and biggest meal of the day. The lord of the manor sat with his most important guests at the "high" table, raised on a dais, or platform, at one end of the great hall. From here, he could look down on the lesser diners and members of his household sitting at the "low" tables. A feast might have three courses of cooked meats and fish, elaborate roasts of swans and peacocks re-clothed in their skins, followed by numerous sweet and spicy dishes. All of these were quickly carried from the nearby kitchen so that they arrived piping hot. The lord was served first, after a sample of the food had been tasted by a servant to make sure it was not poisoned. Only then were the other diners served.

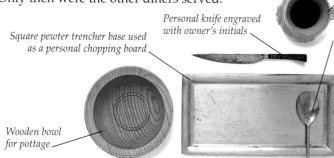

Drinking vessel

Personal knife engraved with owner's initials

Square pewter trencher base used as a personal chopping board

Spoon was provided by the house

Wooden bowl for pottage

GET SET
In the Middle Ages, table forks did not exist, but everyone used their own knife, a spoon, strips of bread, and their fingers to eat very politely, for table manners were important and formed part of every wealthy child's education.

ENTERTAINING IN STYLE
At the high table, the lord sat on a bench at the center with his back to the wall. Guests were seated in order of importance, starting with churchmen, then noblemen, then the lord's family. Servants scurried to and fro with meats, sauces, and jugs of wine from the buttery (bottlery). Singers and acrobats often entertained the diners between courses.

The lord's seat at the center of the table

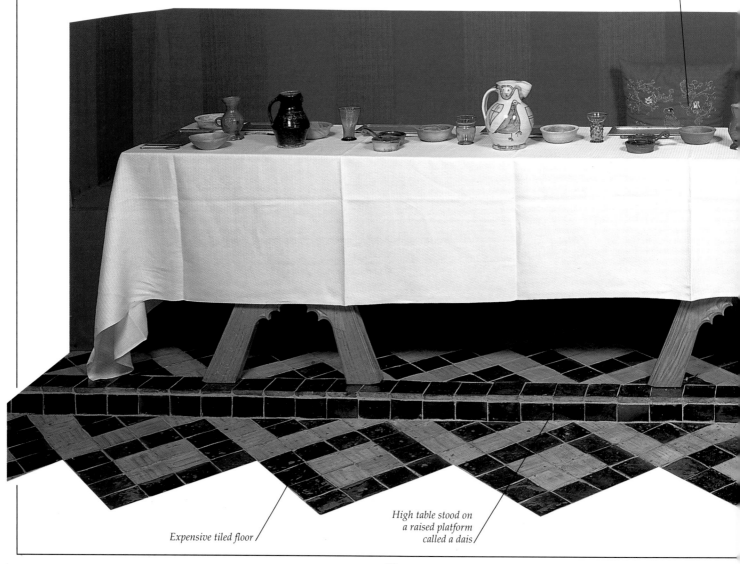

Expensive tiled floor

High table stood on a raised platform called a dais

Large jug for ale

Large wooden platter for serving bread or meat

Horn mug

Leather tankard

Trestle table

Spoons were placed facedown to "keep out the devil"

Hard wooden bench

BANQUET BUSTLE

The banqueting hall could be a crowded, noisy, smelly place. Tables were crammed with diners, and dogs crunched bones on the floor. Only the lord got a serving to himself. Other diners shared a bowl with up to three fellow guests. Most ate with their fingers, so it was important that these were clean and not used for blowing noses or scratching. Table etiquette was strict: "If it happen that you cannot help scratching," one writer advised, "then courteously take a portion of your dress, and scratch with that."

COMMON FARE

Diners seated at a low table would have eaten less elaborate food than that served up for the lord, but there were some common foods. Pottage, a thick broth of vegetables and meat stock, was a staple, everyday dish often served as a first course at feasts. Apart from pottage, everyone ate bread. All food was served on thick slices of stale bread called trenchers, and small loaves called manchets were used for mopping up gravy.

Expensive wine glass

Wooden drinking bowl

Glazed ceramic drinking vessel

Decorated ceramic jug for wine or ale

"Double-salt" for salt and mustard

Dyed cloth wall-cover

Linen tablecloth was "ironed" while damp using round glass linen smoothers

LAID FOR A LORD

The high table was carefully set out with a clean linen tablecloth, trencher bases, pottage and drinking bowls, salt, jugs, and, if the household was wealthy, fine glasses. In the 15th century, a large communal napkin called the long towel was spread over the knees of the diners once they were seated.

The entertainers

Hood to keep bird in the dark

Thick glove protects falconer from the bird's sharp talons

Leather jesses keep bird on the fist

LIFE IN A CASTLE was not all work and warfare. Hunting and hawking were greatly enjoyed by all and brought useful additions for meals. Some outdoor pastimes were quite dangerous – there were tournaments for the knights, and bouts of wrestling or rough ball games. Adults even played children's games such as blindman's bluff, during which a person's head was covered and he or she had to chase the other players. To while away the hours indoors, people played board games and listened to musicians or storytellers. The storytellers recited the great heroic epics of champions such as Roland, troubadours in southern France sang of their love for ladies, and chivalric romances, such as tales of King Arthur's knights, were also popular. Much of this entertainment was provided by traveling minstrels and players, who moved around, but some kings and nobles kept a jester, or clown, to entertain them.

GAMBLERS
Men often gambled at dice and became addicted to it.

ROYAL PLEASURE
This lead badge shows a king riding with his falcon. All ranks of society enjoyed falconry, although some species of bird were reserved for the nobility. Falconry was a skill that had to be learned, but great pleasure was taken in working birds with a decoy bird (or lure) and watching their soaring flight and their ability to plummet down through the air to seize their prey.

BIRD IN THE HAND
People often had close relationships with their falcons. A lord might keep a falcon in his chamber, although they were usually kept in special buildings called mews. Some of the equipment used in falconry, such as the hood, came to Europe from the Middle East at the time of the crusades.

HAWK BELLS
Bells were attached to the bird's leg so that the falconer knew where the creature was.

GARDENER'S WORLD
Castle gardens were usually well tended, not least because they grew herbs and fruit for the table. They were also pleasant places for lords and ladies to stroll and talk.

BEATING TIME
The merrier medieval tunes had a strong drum beat, which sometimes had a complex pattern. These small drums, in a picture from the mid-14th-century Luttrell Psalter (Psalms), are called nakers. A very large drum was sometimes carried on the back while someone else struck it.

Wooden pipe

MINSTREL
A 15th-century musician plays a hornpipe, so-called because its wooden pipe is connected by a leather band to a hollowed-out cow's horn. Dancing to the accompaniment of musicians playing instruments like this was very popular. The earliest forms involved everyone holding hands in a ring or a long chain. Later there were more dances for couples. Minstrels also sang, sometimes accompanied only by the harp. Early songs often dealt with war; later, love songs and songs with a religious theme became popular. There were some songs that reminded people how Jerusalem was ruled by Muslims and urged Christian crusades to win it back.

Slashed sleeves

Leather band

Hollowed-out cow's horn

Checkered pattern often worn by entertainers

HURDY-GURDY
A 14th-century musician is playing a hurdy-gurdy. This was played by turning a handle which sounded all the strings at once to produce a drone-like sound. The fingers of the other hand were then used to produce the required notes.

Woollen tights

WHAT A FOOL
The job of the fool or jester was to make people laugh. He might wear a cap and bells and carry a bladder on a stick (the slapstick), and his jokes could be very crude. He was sometimes allowed to say things to his master that others dared not.

BALL GAMES
This 15th-century ball game with curved sticks may be an early version of hockey. The ball used was quite large and was probably made of leather.

The castle at peace

THE CASTLE DID NOT JUST house a garrison – it was home for the knight and his household. The most important building inside the castle was the great hall, where everyone ate meals, and day-to-day business was done. Sometimes there were private rooms for the lord. There was also a kitchen (often outdoors because of the danger of fire), a chapel, armorer's workshop, blacksmith, stables, kennels, pens for animals, and large storerooms to keep the castle well stocked. A water supply was vital; a well, usable in times of siege, was preferred. Outer walls might be whitewashed to protect against the weather; inner walls could be plastered and painted in attractive colors. Castles were useful resting places for nobles who were traveling. When they were expected, the rooms were made ready and the floors might be covered with fresh straw, rushes, or sweet-smelling grasses.

SONG AND DANCE
Music was welcomed as entertainment and to accompany meals. Dances usually involved many people, often holding hands for types of ring dance.

Coat-of-arms

WALL SCONCE
Only the rich could afford wax candles to burn in sconces like this 16th-century French example. Made of gilt copper, it bears the coat-of-arms of the Castelnau-LaLoubere family encircled by the collar of the Order of St. Michael.

SILVER CRUET
This silver vessel was kept in the chapel to hold the holy water or wine used in the Mass. It was made in Burgundy in the late 14th century.

AT THE LORD'S TABLE
At mealtimes the whole household would come together in the great hall. On this manuscript of about 1316, Lancelot entertains King Arthur by telling him about his adventures.

Limoges enamel decoration

SPIKED
This type of candlestick, called a pricket candlestick, had a long spike to hold the candle. This one, dating to about 1230, was probably used in a castle chapel.

A GAME OF CHESS
King Francis I of France plays chess with Margaret of Angoulême in a picture of about 1504. Being a war game, chess was popular with knights. Chess pieces were often made of beautifully carved bone or ivory.

BLAZING FIRE
Large fireplaces could be set in the thick stone walls of castles. The woman is spinning woolen thread.

Painted and tooled leather sheath

HAND BASIN
Pairs of basins like this, called gemellions, were used to wash peoples' hands at the table. A servant would pour water over the person's hands from one basin into the other and then dry the hands with a towel. Sometimes the water was poured from a ewer (pitcher) instead. This gemellion is decorated with Limoges enamels.

A knight kneels before his lady

Household musician

SERVING KNIVES
Pairs of broad-bladed knives like these 15th-century German ones were used for serving food. Each handle is mounted in brass and the grips have mahogany panels with plaques of stag horn. Each blade has an ancient swastika symbol. The leather sheath has lost its cap.

PLAY THE GAME
Board games helped to pass long evenings. Here a young man of the early 14th century plays checkers with a lady. Backgammon was also popular.

CHAMBER POT
Richer people might use chamber pots, like this one, for convenience, although castles often had lavatories built into the walls. These consisted of a seat connected to a shute which opened directly on to the outside of the castle wall.

Steelyard weight

BRONZE WEIGHTS
The late-13th-century steelyard weight was hung from a pivoting metal arm to figure out the weight of an object placed on the other end. The weight on the right has the English royal arms in the version used after 1405.

Royal arms

Making a knight

WHEN HE WAS ABOUT SEVEN a boy of noble birth who was going to become a knight was usually sent away to a nobleman's household, often that of his uncle or a great lord, to be a page. Here he learned how to behave and how to ride. At about 14 he was apprenticed to a knight whom he served as a squire. He was taught how to handle weapons and how to look after his master's armor and horses; he even went into battle with the knight, helping him to put on his armor and assisting him if he was hurt or unhorsed. He learned how to shoot a bow and to carve meat for food. Successful squires were knighted when they were around 21 years old.

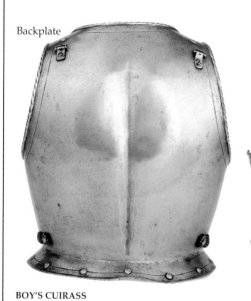

Backplate

BOY'S CUIRASS
These pieces of armor of about 1600 are part of a full armor custom-made to fit a boy. Only rich families could afford to give their young sons such a gift.

Breastplate

*Holes to attach
tassets (thigh pieces)*

THE PAGE
Sons of noble families who were sent away at a very early age to the household of a great lord or to the king's court learned a variety of skills. They were trained to serve a knight, to attend noble ladies, and to learn the art of courtly manners and good behaviour.

PRACTICE MAKES PERFECT
Young men who wanted to be knights had to keep fit. So squires trained constantly to exercise their muscles and improve their skill with weapons. They practiced with each other and also sometimes with their knightly masters, who also needed to keep in shape. Such training was hard and not everyone could manage it. Those who did eventually went on to become knights. This 15th-century picture shows various ways the young men could train.

Putting (throwing) the stone

Throwing the javelin

Acrobatics

Fighting with sword and buckler

Wrestling

Fighting with quarterstaff

THE SQUIRE

The word "squire" comes from the French word *écuyer*, which meant "shield-bearer." In the 11th and 12th centuries many squires seem to have been servants of a lower social class, but later the sons of noble families became squires before being knighted. In the 13th century becoming a knight was so expensive that many young men tried to avoid actually being knighted and remained squires. Later "squire" came to mean a gentleman who owned land.

CHAUCER'S SQUIRE *above*
Geoffrey Chaucer wrote his *Canterbury Tales* in the late 1300s. One of the stories is told by a squire, who is the lively son of a knight and about 20 years old. He can compose songs, dance, draw, and write. He is also a good rider and knows how to joust. Other stories show that some squires were not as well-mannered as Chaucer's. Sometimes they behaved like thugs. At Boston, England, in 1288, two gangs of squires, pretending to hold a squires' tournament, burnt down half the town.

AT THE PEL
Squires could practice against a pel, or wooden post. Sometimes they were given weapons double the weight of those used in battle; this got them used to weapons, and developed their muscles.

AT THE TABLE
Chaucer notes how the squire carved the meat in front of his father at the dining table. Knowing how to carve properly was a skill taught to these sons of noble families as a part of their training.

Thigh-length leather boots

JOUSTING PRACTICE *above*
This could be done with a wooden structure called a quintain, sometimes shaped like a soldier. After striking the shield at the end of one swinging arm the rider had to pass by quickly to avoid the swinging weight.

DUBBING
A squire was finally made into a knight at the ceremony of dubbing. This was originally a blow to the neck with the hand; by the 13th century the blow was replaced by a tap with the sword. The knight's sword and spurs were fastened on, and celebrations might follow when he could show off his skills. Another knight, often the squire's master or even the king, performed the dubbing.

Iron, iron, everywhere

THE MAIN BODY ARMOR worn by early knights was made of mail, consisting of many small, linked iron rings. During the 12th century, knights started to wear more mail; their sleeves got longer, and mail leggings became popular. A padded garment called an aketon was also worn below the mail to absorb blows. In the 14th century knights added steel plates to protect their limbs, and the body was often protected further with a coat-of-plates, made of pieces of iron riveted to a cloth covering. By about 1400 some knights wore full suits of plate armor. A suit weighed about 44-55 lb (20-25 kg), and the weight was spread over the body so that a fit man could run, lie down, or mount a horse unaided in his armor. Stories of cranes being used to winch knights into the saddle are pure fantasy. But armor did have one major drawback: The wearer quickly became very hot.

MAIL
In this piece of mail, each open ring is interlinked with four others and closed with a rivet. A mail coat weighed about 20-31 lb (9-14 kg), and most of the weight was taken on the knight's shoulders. As mail was flexible, a heavy blow could cause broken bones or bruising.

KNIGHTLY PLAQUE
This mounted knight of the 14th century has a helm fitted with a crest. This helped to identify him in battle. However, by this time headgear like this was losing popularity in favor of the basinet and visor.

MAIL MAKER
No one knows exactly how mail was made. This 15th-century picture shows an armorer using pliers to join the links. Garments were shaped by increasing or reducing the number of links in each row, rather like stiches in modern knitting.

Pin allowing visor to be removed

Cord allowing mail to be removed

BASINET
This Italian basinet of the late 14th century was originally fitted with a visor that pivoted over the brow. But, probably within the helmet's working life, a side-pivoting visor was fitted. The Germans called this type of helmet a *Hundsgugel* (hound's hood).

Ventilation holes

Modern mail neck guard

COURTLY GAUNTLETS
Gauntlet plates, like this late-14th-century pair from Milan, Italy, were riveted to the back of a leather glove. Smaller plates were added to protect the fingers. On these plates each cuff has a band of brass on which is written the latin word *AMOR*, love.

SALLET
Light horsemen, who might not wear armor on their lower legs, often wore helmets like this German sallet of 1480-1510. It was originally fitted with a chin strap.

Visor with horizontal sight

THE COMING OF PLATE ARMOR
The knight on the left dates from about 1340. Over his padded aketon he wears a mail coat and over that a coat-of-plates. His surcoat is short and his legs have some plate armor. The knight on the right dates from about 1420 and has full plate armor.

"Gothic-style" fluted decoration

BARBUTE
Italian barbutes, like this one of about 1445, look rather like ancient Greek Corinthian helmets. The rosette-headed rivets secured a canvas lining and inside, to which was sewn a padded lining. Rivets lower down originally held a leather chin strap to keep the helmet from being knocked off.

UNHORSED
Fully mailed knights needed to protect themselves against heavy blows from lances or maces. This picture, drawn by Matthew Paris in the first half of the 13th century, shows the large shields they used. By 1400, thanks to the effectiveness of plate armor, shields had become much smaller.

Pointed cuff

Center plate

Articulated plates

Shaped knuckle plate

GAUNTLET
This shows the long, fluted style popular for German "Gothic" armor of the later 15th century. The missing finger and thumb plates would be riveted to a glove attached inside. Plate armor like this gave better protection than mail, because it was solid and did not flex when struck by a weapon.

THE MAILED KNIGHT
This knight of about 1250 wears a cloth surcoat over his mail, perhaps in imitation of Muslim dress seen on crusade (pp. 112-113). His mail sleeves are extended into mittens, with leather palms to give a good grip.

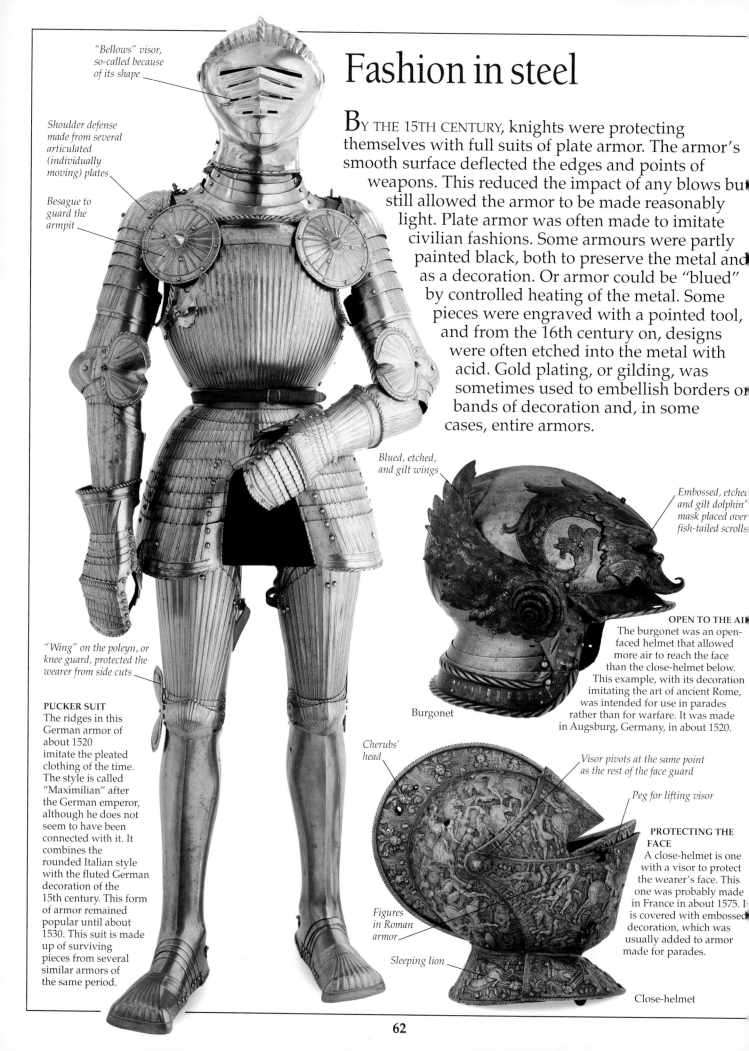

Fashion in steel

B Y THE 15TH CENTURY, knights were protecting themselves with full suits of plate armor. The armor's smooth surface deflected the edges and points of weapons. This reduced the impact of any blows but still allowed the armor to be made reasonably light. Plate armor was often made to imitate civilian fashions. Some armours were partly painted black, both to preserve the metal and as a decoration. Or armor could be "blued" by controlled heating of the metal. Some pieces were engraved with a pointed tool, and from the 16th century on, designs were often etched into the metal with acid. Gold plating, or gilding, was sometimes used to embellish borders or bands of decoration and, in some cases, entire armors.

"Bellows" visor, so-called because of its shape

Shoulder defense made from several articulated (individually moving) plates

Besague to guard the armpit

Blued, etched, and gilt wings

Embossed, etched and gilt dolphin mask placed over fish-tailed scrolls

OPEN TO THE AIR
The burgonet was an open-faced helmet that allowed more air to reach the face than the close-helmet below. This example, with its decoration imitating the art of ancient Rome, was intended for use in parades rather than for warfare. It was made in Augsburg, Germany, in about 1520.

Burgonet

"Wing" on the poleyn, or knee guard, protected the wearer from side cuts

PUCKER SUIT
The ridges in this German armor of about 1520 imitate the pleated clothing of the time. The style is called "Maximilian" after the German emperor, although he does not seem to have been connected with it. It combines the rounded Italian style with the fluted German decoration of the 15th century. This form of armor remained popular until about 1530. This suit is made up of surviving pieces from several similar armors of the same period.

Cherubs' head

Visor pivots at the same point as the rest of the face guard

Peg for lifting visor

PROTECTING THE FACE
A close-helmet is one with a visor to protect the wearer's face. This one was probably made in France in about 1575. It is covered with embossed decoration, which was usually added to armor made for parades.

Figures in Roman armor

Sleeping lion

Close-helmet

Gorget plates attached to the buffe protect the throat

Slim plates on this falling buffe may be lowered over one another to allow more air to reach the face

Large pauldrons made of several strips of steel joined internally by leather straps, which let them move

Lance rest helped support the weight of the lance and keep it from being rammed through the armpit on impact

Reinforcing breast (plackart) attached to the breastplate to increase protection against firearms

Small plates on the gauntlets give complete freedom of movement to the hand

Poleyn has plates above and below, which allow the knee to bend without exposing the cloth beneath

LATEST FASHION
This armor was made for Lord Buckhurst in about 1587. It is a product of the workshops in Greenwich set up by Henry VIII. The breastplate has followed the fashion in becoming more and more pointed at the waist until, as here, the full shape known as a peascod is formed. The bulging hips allow for thick underwear worn beneath. The burgonet has a triple-barred face-guard behind a removable buffe.

Flexible sabaton leaves the sole exposed so the shoe beneath does not skid

TRIUMPHAL ENTRY
This picture of King Louis XII of France entering Quenes was painted about 1510. The colored cloth skirts popular at the time were called bases. The king's helmet is fitted with a heraldic crest.

MASTER DRAWING
Jacob Halder, who was master armourer at Greenwich, near London, produced illustrations for people who wanted armor made. They were often in the form of a set of pieces called a garniture which could be made into armors for war and tournament. This one was for Sir Henry Lee, master of the armouries from 1578 to 1610.

ON PARADE
Three knights ride in procession, from the early 16th-century *Triumph of Maximilian*. They carry enormous parade banners representing Styria, Austria, and Old Austria. The horses wear plate armor; the animal in the middle even has pieces to guard his upper legs – such items were very rare.

Armor, the inside story

PEOPLE OFTEN THINK that plate armor is clumsy and stiff. But if it were, it would be little use on the battlefield. In fact, a man in armor could do just about anything a man can do when not wearing it. The secret lies in the way armorers made the plates so that they could move with each other and with the wearer. Some plates were attached to each other with a rivet, which allowed the two parts to pivot (turn) at that point. Others were joined by a sliding rivet, one part of which was set not in a round hole but in a slot, so the two plates could move in and out. Internal leather connecting straps, called leathers, also allowed this type of movement. Tube-shaped plates could also have "flanged" edge, or projecting rim, to fit inside the edge of another tubular plate so that they could twist around.

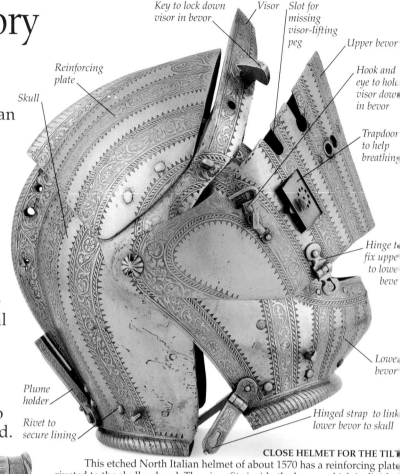

Key to lock down visor in bevor

Visor

Slot for missing visor-lifting peg

Upper bevor

Hook and eye to hold visor down in bevor

Trapdoor to help breathing

Reinforcing plate

Skull

Hinge to fix upper to lower bevor

Lower bevor

Plume holder

Rivet to secure lining

Hinged strap to link lower bevor to skull

CLOSE HELMET FOR THE TILT
This etched North Italian helmet of about 1570 has a reinforcing plate riveted to the skull or bowl. The visor fits inside the bevor, which is divided into upper and lower parts. The visor and the two parts of the bevor all pivot at the same point on each side of the skull and can be locked together.

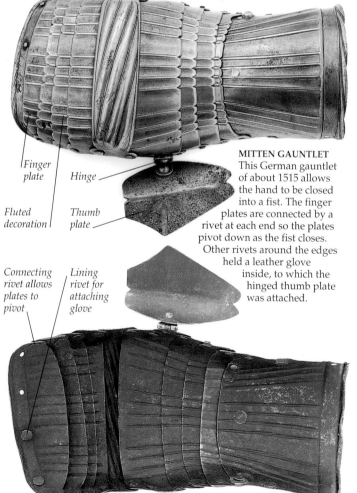

Finger plate

Hinge

Fluted decoration

Thumb plate

MITTEN GAUNTLET
This German gauntlet of about 1515 allows the hand to be closed into a fist. The finger plates are connected by a rivet at each end so the plates pivot down as the fist closes. Other rivets around the edges held a leather glove inside, to which the hinged thumb plate was attached.

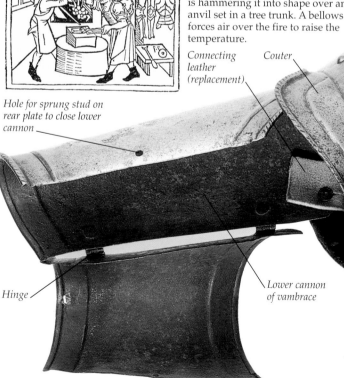

HOT WORK
This armorer has heated a piece of metal in a furnace to soften it and is hammering it into shape over an anvil set in a tree trunk. A bellows forces air over the fire to raise the temperature.

Connecting leather (replacement)

Couter

Hole for sprung stud on rear plate to close lower cannon

Connecting rivet allows plates to pivot

Lining rivet for attaching glove

Hinge

Lower cannon of vambrace

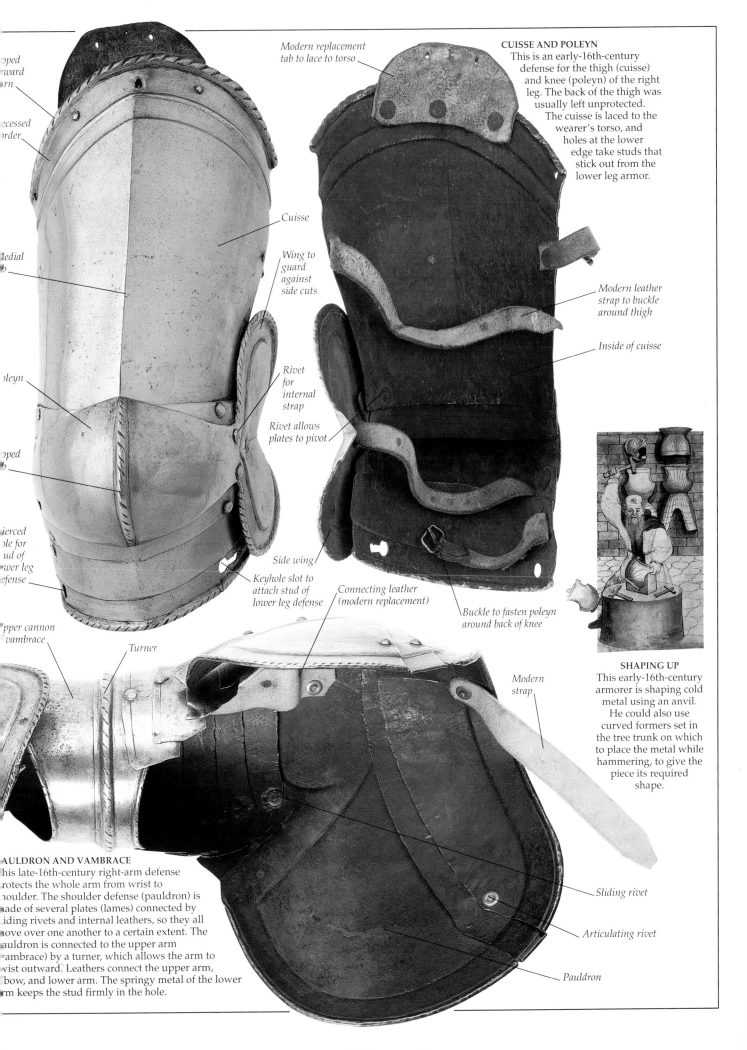

oped
ward
rn

ecessed
order

Medial

oleyn

oped

ierced
le for
ud of
wer leg
efense

pper cannon
vambrace

Cuisse

Medial

*Wing to
guard
against
side cuts*

*Rivet
for
internal
strap*

*Rivet allows
plates to pivot*

Side wing

Keyhole slot to
attach stud of
lower leg defense

Turner

CUISSE AND POLEYN

This is an early-16th-century
defense for the thigh (cuisse)
and knee (poleyn) of the right
leg. The back of the thigh was
usually left unprotected.
The cuisse is laced to the
wearer's torso, and
holes at the lower
edge take studs that
stick out from the
lower leg armor.

*Modern replacement
tab to lace to torso*

*Modern leather
strap to buckle
around thigh*

Inside of cuisse

*Connecting leather
(modern replacement)*

*Buckle to fasten poleyn
around back of knee*

*Modern
strap*

SHAPING UP

This early-16th-century
armorer is shaping cold
metal using an anvil.
He could also use
curved formers set in
the tree trunk on which
to place the metal while
hammering, to give the
piece its required
shape.

Sliding rivet

Articulating rivet

Pauldron

AULDRON AND VAMBRACE

his late-16th-century right-arm defense
rotects the whole arm from wrist to
houlder. The shoulder defense (pauldron) is
ade of several plates (lames) connected by
iding rivets and internal leathers, so they all
ove over one another to a certain extent. The
auldron is connected to the upper arm
vambrace) by a turner, which allows the arm to
wist outward. Leathers connect the upper arm,
bow, and lower arm. The springy metal of the lower
rm keeps the stud firmly in the hole.

Arms and the man

THE SWORD WAS THE most important knightly weapon, a symbol of knighthood itself. Until the late 13th century the double-edged cutting sword was used in battle. But as plate armor became more common more pointed swords became popular, because they were better for thrusting through the gaps between the plates. The mace, which could concuss an opponent, also became more popular. Before drawing his sword or using his mace, however, a mounted knight usually charged at his opponent with his lance lowered. Lances increased in length during the medieval period and, from about 1300, began to be fitted with circular vamplates to guard the hand. Other weapons such as the short ax could be used on horseback, while long-handled staff weapons, held in both hands, could be used on foot.

AT THE READY
The double-edged cutting sword, shown unsheathed in this 13th-century tomb effigy, could tear mail links apart and drive them into a wound.

THE COUCHED LANCE
Early 14th-century knights charge in formation with lances "couched" under their arms. To keep their line, they rode at a trot before charging as they neared the enemy.

SHINING SWORD
This sword of about 1460 has a copper-gilt crossguard. Like the weapon above it, it was probably made for a rich knight.

Copper-gilt crossguard

Fish-tail pommel

Horn grip

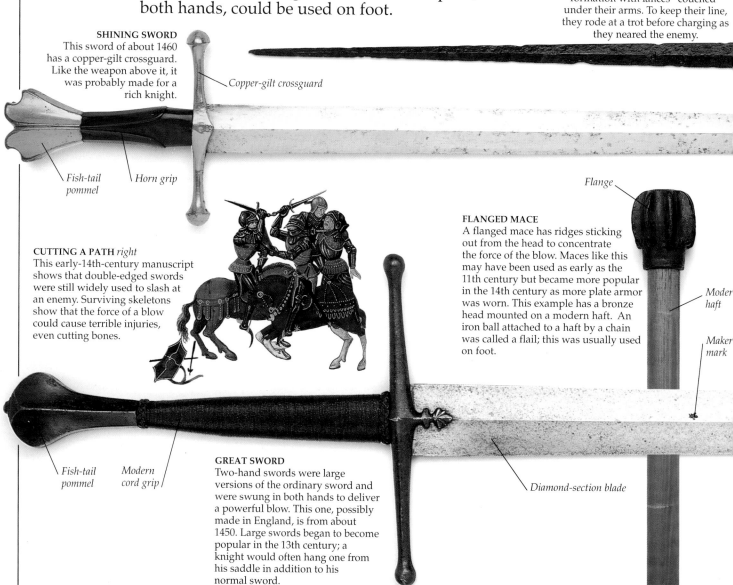

CUTTING A PATH *right*
This early-14th-century manuscript shows that double-edged swords were still widely used to slash at an enemy. Surviving skeletons show that the force of a blow could cause terrible injuries, even cutting bones.

FLANGED MACE
A flanged mace has ridges sticking out from the head to concentrate the force of the blow. Maces like this may have been used as early as the 11th century but became more popular in the 14th century as more plate armor was worn. This example has a bronze head mounted on a modern haft. An iron ball attached to a haft by a chain was called a flail; this was usually used on foot.

Flange

Modern haft

Maker mark

Fish-tail pommel

Modern cord grip

GREAT SWORD
Two-hand swords were large versions of the ordinary sword and were swung in both hands to deliver a powerful blow. This one, possibly made in England, is from about 1450. Large swords began to become popular in the 13th century; a knight would often hang one from his saddle in addition to his normal sword.

Diamond-section blade

Diamond-profile blade

Cross-guard

Modern cord grip

Wheel pommel with cap

GETTING THE POINT
On this sharply pointed war sword of the second half of the 14th century, the old-style blade with a central groove or fuller has been replaced by a stiffer one with a diamond-shaped profile. This assisted the thrust. The acute point could burst apart the links of a piece of mail.

DEATH OR GLORY
Two riders slammed together at about 60 mph (96 km/h); this made the pointed lance lethal. In this early-15th-century picture a knight's lance has passed by his opponent's shield and punched through his armor. The figure on the left has a heavy-bladed cutting sword called a falchion. A pole-ax, a staff weapon used on foot, lies on the ground.

WEAPON OF RANK
This sword was probably made for a wealthy person. Dating from the late 15th century, it has a sunken hollow in the pommel that would have held a plaque with the owner's coat of arms.

Fig-shaped pommel

Hollow for small shield

BLOODY BUSINESS
When a dagger was used the opponent was often grasped around the neck before the fatal blow was struck. This often meant stabbing at the face or, as in this late-15th-century picture, cutting the throat. Like sharply pointed swords, such daggers could also pierce mail.

SHORT AX
Knights sometimes wielded two-handed axes, but the smaller, single-handed variety was easier to use on horseback. This 14th-century example, mounted on a modern haft, has the remains of long iron langets which ran down the haft to stop the ax head being cut off. The back is extended to form a beak.

Part of langet

Single-edged blade

Remains of gilt decoration

Rondel

DAGGER
Knights did not use daggers very much until the 14th century. This is a late-15th-century rondel dagger, so-called because of the protective iron discs at either end of the grip. It was the typical knightly dagger and was carried in a decorated leather sheath.

On horseback

THE HORSE was an expensive but vital part of a knight's equipment. Knights needed horses for warfare, hunting, jousting, traveling, and carrying baggage. The most costly animal was the destrier, or war-horse. This was a stallion about the size of a modern heavy hunter. Its deep chest gave it staying power yet it was also nimble. Knights prized war-horses from Italy, France, and Spain. In fact the Spanish Andalusian is more like a war-horse than any other modern kind is. By the 13th century, knights usually had at least two war-horses, plus other horses for different tasks. The courser was a swift hunting horse, though this name was sometimes applied to the war-horse, with "destrier" used for the jousting horse. For travel, knights often used a well-bred, easy-paced mount called a palfrey. Sumpter horses carried baggage.

FIT FOR A KING
An early-14th-century miniature shows the king of England on his war-horse. The richly decorated covering, or trapper, could be used to display heraldic arms and might be padded for extra protection. Some were even made of mail. Notice the "fan" crest.

GREAT HORSE
A destrier, or "great horse," wears armor on its head, neck, and chest, the latter partly covered in decorative cloth. The knight in this 15th-century picture wears long spurs and shows the straight-legged riding position. He uses double reins, one of which is highly decorated.

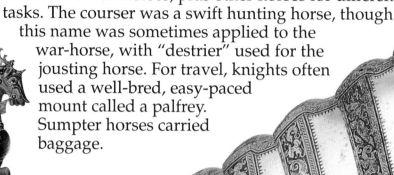

Etched and gilt decoration

Separately moving metal plates

"Eye" for leathers

Tread

MINIATURE GOAD
A knight wore spurs on his feet, and used them to urge on his horse. This 12th- or 13th-century prick spur is made of tin-plated iron. The two leather straps that passed over and under the foot were riveted to the ends of each spur arm.

Prick or goad

Rowel

ROWEL SPUR *right*
Spurs with a rotating spiked rowel on the end of the arm had replaced prick spurs by the early 14th century. This decorated copper-gilt example is from the second half of the 15th century.

FIRM SEAT
Iron stirrups like this one dating from the 14th century were worn with long straps so the knight was almost standing in them. This, together with the support of high saddle boards at front and rear, meant he had a very secure seat from which to fight.

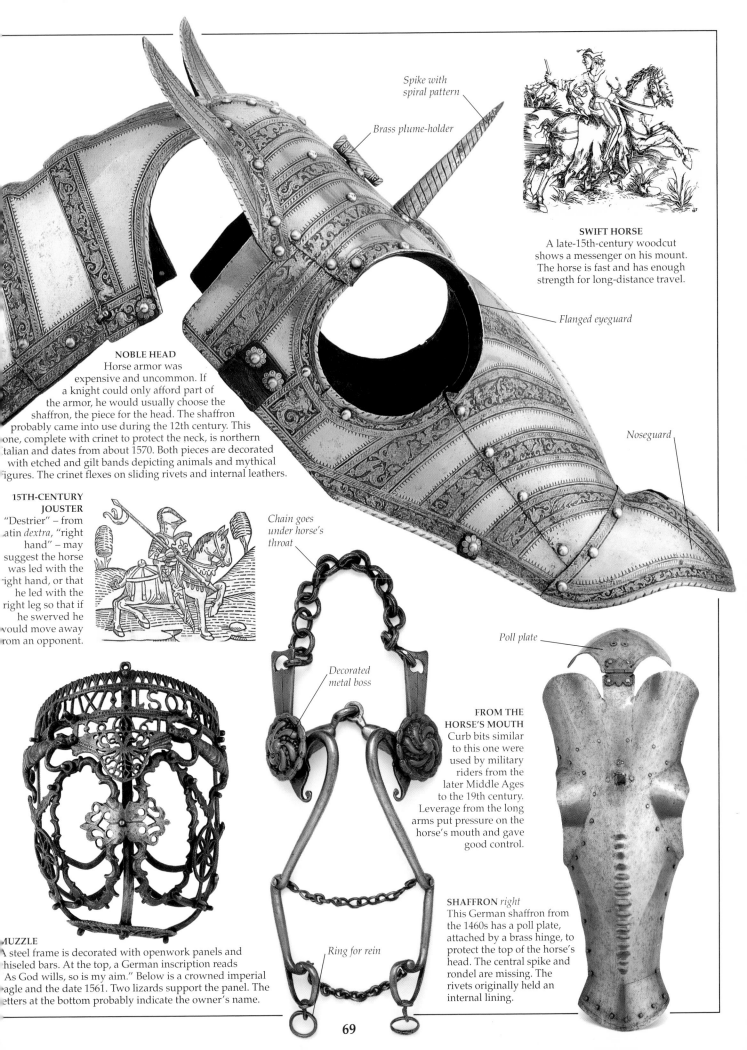

Spike with spiral pattern

Brass plume-holder

SWIFT HORSE
A late-15th-century woodcut shows a messenger on his mount. The horse is fast and has enough strength for long-distance travel.

Flanged eyeguard

NOBLE HEAD
Horse armor was expensive and uncommon. If a knight could only afford part of the armor, he would usually choose the shaffron, the piece for the head. The shaffron probably came into use during the 12th century. This one, complete with crinet to protect the neck, is northern Italian and dates from about 1570. Both pieces are decorated with etched and gilt bands depicting animals and mythical figures. The crinet flexes on sliding rivets and internal leathers.

Noseguard

15TH-CENTURY JOUSTER
"Destrier" – from Latin *dextra*, "right hand" – may suggest the horse was led with the right hand, or that he led with the right leg so that if he swerved he would move away from an opponent.

Chain goes under horse's throat

Decorated metal boss

Poll plate

FROM THE HORSE'S MOUTH
Curb bits similar to this one were used by military riders from the later Middle Ages to the 19th century. Leverage from the long arms put pressure on the horse's mouth and gave good control.

MUZZLE
A steel frame is decorated with openwork panels and chiseled bars. At the top, a German inscription reads "As God wills, so is my aim." Below is a crowned imperial eagle and the date 1561. Two lizards support the panel. The letters at the bottom probably indicate the owner's name.

Ring for rein

SHAFFRON *right*
This German shaffron from the 1460s has a poll plate, attached by a brass hinge, to protect the top of the horse's head. The central spike and rondel are missing. The rivets originally held an internal lining.

The ideal of chivalry

Aʟᴛʜᴏᴜɢʜ ᴋɴɪɢʜᴛꜱ were men of war, they traditionally behaved in a courteous and civil way when dealing with their enemies. In the 12th century this kind of behavior was extended to form a knightly code of conduct, with a special emphasis on courtly manners toward women. The poems of courtly love recited by the troubadours of southern France were based on this code, and the romance stories that became popular in the 13th century showed the ways a warrior should behave.

Churchmen liked the idea of high standards and made the knighting ceremony a religious occasion with a church vigil and purifiying bath (pp. 58-59). Books on chivalry also appeared, though in reality knights often found it difficult to live up to the ideal.

GEORGE AND THE DRAGON
St. George was a soldier martyred (put to death because of his religion) by the Romans in about A.D. 350. During the Middle Ages stories appeared telling how he rescued a king's daughter from a dragon. He became especially connected with England. This carved ivory shows St. George with the battlements of a castle in the background.

KNIGHT IN SHINING ARMOR
This 15th-century tournament parade shield depicts a bareheaded knight kneeling before his lady. The words on the scroll mean "You or death," and the figure of death is represented by a skeleton.

TRUE-LOVE KNOTS
Medallions like this were sometimes made to mark special occasions, such as marriages. This one was struck to comemorate the marriage of Margaret of Austria to the Duke of Savoy in 1502. The knots in the background are the badge of Savoy – they also refer to the way the couple's love will unite the two families.

WHAT'S IN A NAME?
This scene, from the 15th-century book *The Lovelorn Heart*, by Frenchman René of Anjou, illustrates the strange world of the medieval romance in which people can stand for objects or feelings. Here the knight, called Cueur (meaning Heart), reads an inscription while his companion, Desire, lies sleeping.

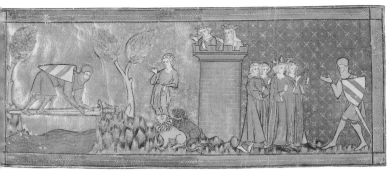

LANCELOT AND GUINEVERE
King Arthur was probably a fifth-century warrior, but the legends of the king and the knights of the Round Table gained popularity in 13th-century Europe. They tell of Arthur's struggles against evil and of the love between Arthur's queen, Guinevere, and Sir Lancelot, which eventually led to the destruction of Arthur's court. In this story, Lancelot crosses a sword bridge to rescue Guinevere.

THE KNIGHT OF THE CART
Knights rode on horseback and it was usually thought a disgrace for a knight to travel in a cart. This picture shows an episode from the story of Sir Lancelot. Lancelot was famous for his valour and skill in combat, but his love affair with Queen Guinevere brought him shame. In this episode Lancelot meets a dwarf who offers to tell him where Guinevere is if he will ride in the cart.

ROYAL CHAMPION
Sir Edward Dymoke was the champion of Queen Elizabeth I. At her coronation banquet in Westminster, it was his job to ride fully armed into the hall and hurl his gauntlet to the ground to defy anyone who wished to question the queen's right to rule. Such a challenge was made at every English coronation until that of George IV in 1821.

Lock

Corner reinforcement

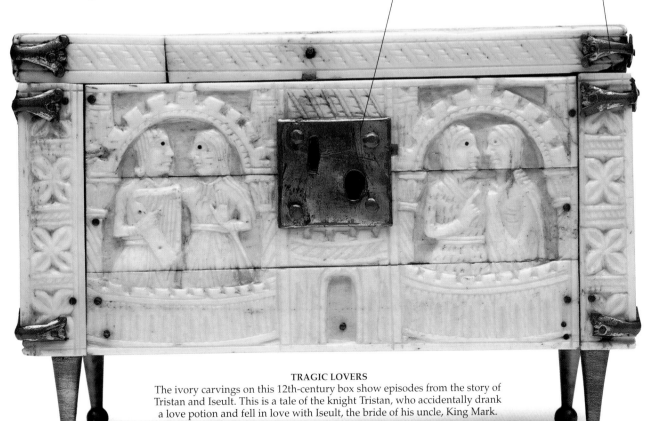

TRAGIC LOVERS
The ivory carvings on this 12th-century box show episodes from the story of Tristan and Iseult. This is a tale of the knight Tristan, who accidentally drank a love potion and fell in love with Iseult, the bride of his uncle, King Mark.

The tournament

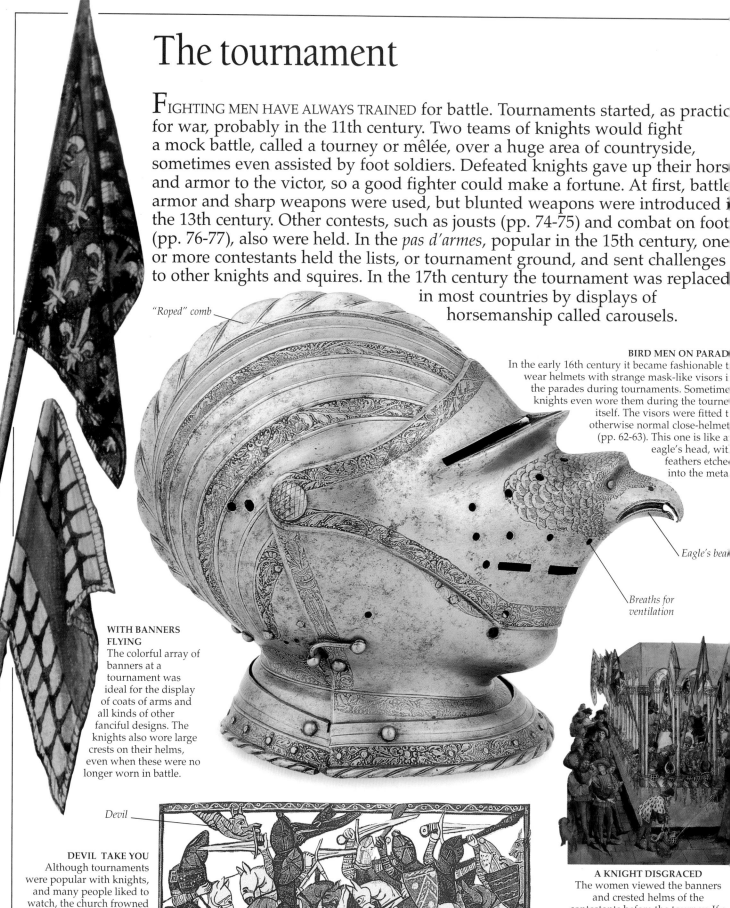

FIGHTING MEN HAVE ALWAYS TRAINED for battle. Tournaments started, as practic for war, probably in the 11th century. Two teams of knights would fight a mock battle, called a tourney or mêlée, over a huge area of countryside, sometimes even assisted by foot soldiers. Defeated knights gave up their hors and armor to the victor, so a good fighter could make a fortune. At first, battle armor and sharp weapons were used, but blunted weapons were introduced i the 13th century. Other contests, such as jousts (pp. 74-75) and combat on foot (pp. 76-77), also were held. In the *pas d'armes*, popular in the 15th century, one or more contestants held the lists, or tournament ground, and sent challenges to other knights and squires. In the 17th century the tournament was replaced in most countries by displays of horsemanship called carousels.

"Roped" comb

BIRD MEN ON PARAD
In the early 16th century it became fashionable t wear helmets with strange mask-like visors i the parades during tournaments. Sometime knights even wore them during the tourne itself. The visors were fitted t otherwise normal close-helmet (pp. 62-63). This one is like a eagle's head, wit feathers etche into the meta

Eagle's bea

Breaths for ventilation

WITH BANNERS FLYING
The colorful array of banners at a tournament was ideal for the display of coats of arms and all kinds of other fanciful designs. The knights also wore large crests on their helms, even when these were no longer worn in battle.

Devil

DEVIL TAKE YOU
Although tournaments were popular with knights, and many people liked to watch, the church frowned on them because much blood was often spilled. In this early-14th-century picture, devils wait to seize the souls of knights killed in a tourney.

A KNIGHT DISGRACED
The women viewed the banners and crested helms of the contestants before the tourney. If a lady knew that one of the knights had done wrong, his helm was taken down and he was banned from the lists. This picture comes from the 15th-century tournament book of René of Anjou.

CLUB TOURNEY
In a club tourney, two teams using blunt swords and clubs tried to knock the crests off their opponents' helmets, which were fitted with protective face grilles. Each knight had a banner-bearer, and attendants (called varlets) stood ready in case the knight fell. In this picture, the knight of honor rides between two ropes that separate the teams; ladies and judges are in the stands. The lists were small, but the artist has compressed everything to fit the picture.

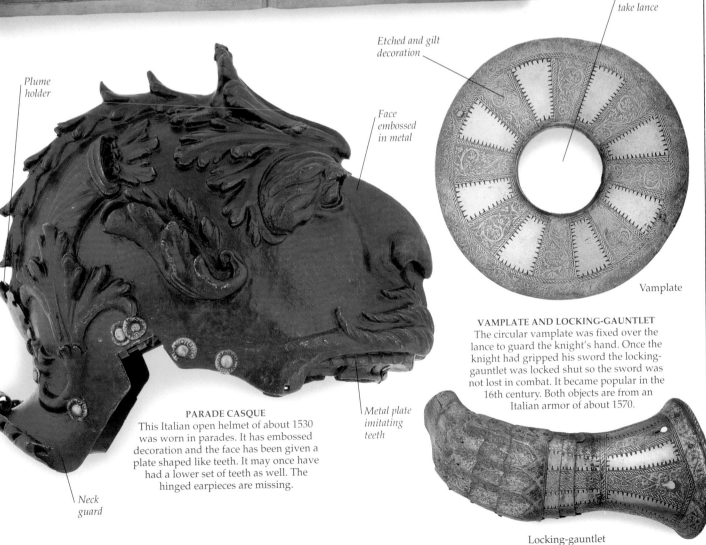

Plume holder

Etched and gilt decoration

Hole to take lance

Face embossed in metal

Vamplate

VAMPLATE AND LOCKING-GAUNTLET
The circular vamplate was fixed over the lance to guard the knight's hand. Once the knight had gripped his sword the locking-gauntlet was locked shut so the sword was not lost in combat. It became popular in the 16th century. Both objects are from an Italian armor of about 1570.

PARADE CASQUE
This Italian open helmet of about 1530 was worn in parades. It has embossed decoration and the face has been given a plate shaped like teeth. It may once have had a lower set of teeth as well. The hinged earpieces are missing.

Metal plate imitating teeth

Neck guard

Locking-gauntlet

The joust

URING THE 13TH CENTURY a dramatic new element was added to the tournament – jousts, in which knights fought one-on-one. In a joust, a knight could show his skill without other contestants getting in the way. Usually the knights fought on horseback with lances, though in some contests they continued the fight with swords. Two knights would charge toward each other at top speed and try to unhorse each other with a single blow of the lance. You could also score points if you broke your lance on your opponent's shield. In "jousts of war" knights used sharp lances. These could kill a knight, so many jousters preferred "jousts of peace," using a lance fitted with a blunt tip or with a "coronel" shaped like a small crown to spread the impact. Special armor was developed for jousting, to increase protection. A barrier called the tilt was introduced in the 15th century to separate the knights and avoid collisions.

Eye slit

FROG-MOUTHED HELM
This 15th-century helmet for the jousts of peace was originally fastened down the back and front. The wearer could see his opponent by leaning forward during the charge. At the moment of impact he straightened up, so that the "frog-mouthed" lower lip protected his eyes from the lance head or fragments of the shaft.

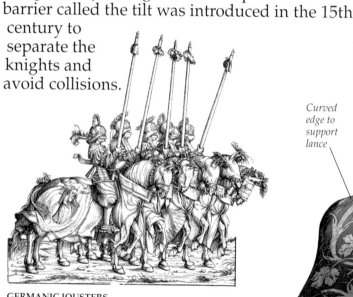

GERMANIC JOUSTERS
In the Germanic countries, knights often practised the *Rennen*, a version of the jousts of war. As no barrier was used, the knights' legs were partially protected by metal shields.

Curved edge to support lance

LANCER'S SHIELD
This late 15th-century wooden shield is covered in leather. It was probably used for the *Rennen*. The lance could be placed in the recess in the side. The shield was attached to the breastplate by a staple nailed to the rear.

BREAKING A LANCE
Lances were made of wood and by the 16th century were often fluted to help them splinter easily. This 17th-century lance is slightly thinner than those used for jousting against an opponent. It was used to spear a small ring hanging from a bracket.

PARADE BEFORE THE TILT
Knights paraded beside the tilt, or barrier, before the jousting commenced. This scene from Jean Froissart's *Chronicles* was painted in the late 15th century, though it depicts the jousts at St. Inglevert, which took place in 1390, before the tilt was introduced. Attendants with spare lances accompany the knights.

74

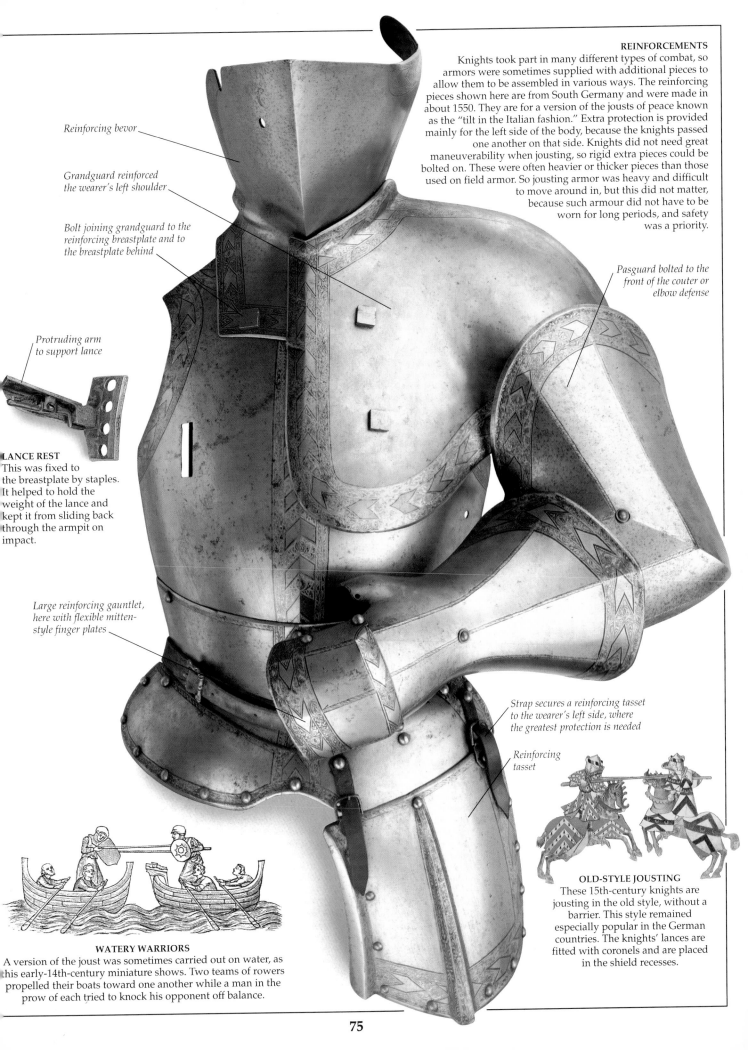

Reinforcing bevor

Grandguard reinforced the wearer's left shoulder

Bolt joining grandguard to the reinforcing breastplate and to the breastplate behind

Protruding arm to support lance

LANCE REST
This was fixed to the breastplate by staples. It helped to hold the weight of the lance and kept it from sliding back through the armpit on impact.

Large reinforcing gauntlet, here with flexible mitten-style finger plates

REINFORCEMENTS
Knights took part in many different types of combat, so armors were sometimes supplied with additional pieces to allow them to be assembled in various ways. The reinforcing pieces shown here are from South Germany and were made in about 1550. They are for a version of the jousts of peace known as the "tilt in the Italian fashion." Extra protection is provided mainly for the left side of the body, because the knights passed one another on that side. Knights did not need great maneuverability when jousting, so rigid extra pieces could be bolted on. These were often heavier or thicker pieces than those used on field armor. So jousting armor was heavy and difficult to move around in, but this did not matter, because such armour did not have to be worn for long periods, and safety was a priority.

Pasguard bolted to the front of the couter or elbow defense

Strap secures a reinforcing tasset to the wearer's left side, where the greatest protection is needed

Reinforcing tasset

OLD-STYLE JOUSTING
These 15th-century knights are jousting in the old style, without a barrier. This style remained especially popular in the German countries. The knights' lances are fitted with coronels and are placed in the shield recesses.

WATERY WARRIORS
A version of the joust was sometimes carried out on water, as this early-14th-century miniature shows. Two teams of rowers propelled their boats toward one another while a man in the prow of each tried to knock his opponent off balance.

Foot combat

IN SOME 13TH-CENTURY jousts the knights dismounted after using their lances and continued fighting with swords. By the 14th century, such foot combats were popular in their own right. Contestants took turns delivering blows, and men-at-arms stood ready to separate fighters who got too excited. From 15th-century writings we learn that each man sometimes threw a javelin first, then fought with sword, ax, or staff weapon. Later still, such combats were replaced by contests in which two teams fought across a barrier. These contests were called foot tournaments because, as in the mounted tourney (pp. 72-73), each man tried to break a spear against his opponent before continuing the fight with blunted swords.

AT THE READY
This detail from a 16th-century Flemish tapestry shows contestants waiting to take part in foot combat over the barrier. A page is handing one knight his helmet.

Sword cuts

Visor

Holes for laces of cross straps to hold the head inside

Chin piece

CLOSE-HELMET
This helmet was designed for the tournament on foot. It is so richly gilded that it is surprising that it was ever worn in actual combat. But the sword cuts show that it must have been used. It was part of a dazzling garniture of gilt armor made in 1555.

FORMAL FIGHT
Foot combats in the 15th century took place without a barrier, so the contestants protected their legs with armor. The most common helmet for these contests was the great basinet (pp. 60-61), which was outdated for war by the middle of the century.

Hand-threaded screw

BROW REINFORCE
This plate was screwed to the visor of the close-helmet shown on the right. It gave more protection to the left side of the head.

Hole for hearing

Visor

Bevor

Pivoting fork for holding up bevor

ARMET
In this type of helmet the cheek-pieces pivot outward when it is put on, instead of the front half of the helmet swinging up as in the helmet at top right. This German example of about 1535 has a visor that fits inside the rim of the bevor, where it is held by a spring-catch. The bevor is locked over the cheek piece in the same way.

Eyeslit

Lifting peg

EXCHANGE VISOR
Two threaded bolts allowed the visor to be removed from the helmet on the left and replaced with this one, which has a number of ventilation holes. It could be used for battle or for foot combat.

TRIAL BY BATTLE
Not all foot contests were held for sport. Sometimes a charge of murder or treason was settled by a combat, in which God was thought to help the innocent man. The contest went on until one was either killed or surrendered, in which case he was executed.

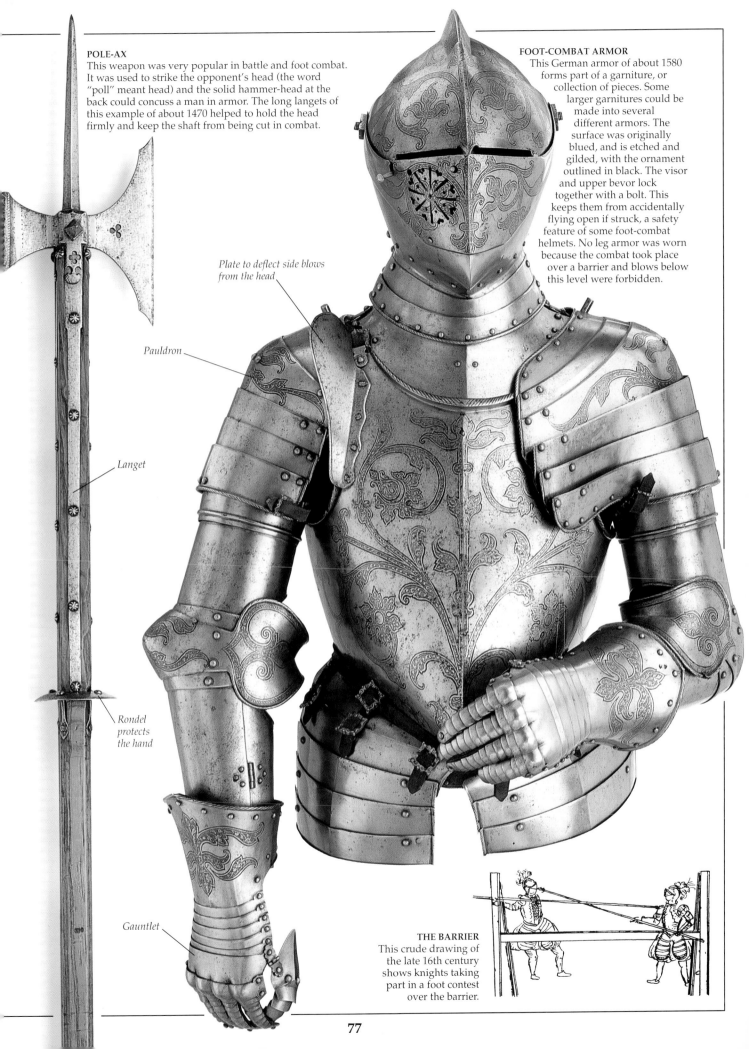

POLE-AX
This weapon was very popular in battle and foot combat. It was used to strike the opponent's head (the word "poll" meant head) and the solid hammer-head at the back could concuss a man in armor. The long langets of this example of about 1470 helped to hold the head firmly and keep the shaft from being cut in combat.

FOOT-COMBAT ARMOR
This German armor of about 1580 forms part of a garniture, or collection of pieces. Some larger garnitures could be made into several different armors. The surface was originally blued, and is etched and gilded, with the ornament outlined in black. The visor and upper bevor lock together with a bolt. This keeps them from accidentally flying open if struck, a safety feature of some foot-combat helmets. No leg armor was worn because the combat took place over a barrier and blows below this level were forbidden.

Plate to deflect side blows from the head

Pauldron

Langet

Rondel protects the hand

Gauntlet

THE BARRIER
This crude drawing of the late 16th century shows knights taking part in a foot contest over the barrier.

Heraldry

Or, a pale gules

Azure, a fess embattled or

Sable, a cross engrailed or

Lozengy, argent and gules

Vert, a crescent or

Azure, a fleur- de-lys or

Gules, a spur argent

Mᴇɴ ʜᴀᴠᴇ ᴀʟᴡᴀʏs decorated their shields. In the 12th century these designs became more standardized in a system known as heraldry, which enabled a knight to be identified by symbols on his shield, or a full coat of arms. It is often said that this was done because helmets with face guards made knights difficult to recognize, but a more likely reason was the need to identify contestants in tournaments. Heraldry was based on strict rules. Only one coat of arms was carried by a knight, and this passed to his eldest son when he died. Other children used variants of their father's arms. Arms used a series of standard colors and "metals" (silver or gold) and are described in a special language, based on Old French.

BADGE OF OFFICE
This copper arm badge was worn by a servant of François de Lorraine, Hospitaler Prior of France from 1549 to 1563, whose arms it bears. Retainers of a lord often wore his livery badge.

COSTUME DESIGN
The fleur-de-lys, heraldic emblem of France, is used to decorate this long tunic. The fur lining of the mantle was also adapted for heraldic purposes.

ROLL OF ARMS
Heralds made lists to keep a record of participants in military events like tournaments and battles. The Carlisle Roll contains 277 shields of King Edward III's retinue on his visit to Carlisle, England, in 1334.

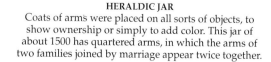

HERALDIC JAR
Coats of arms were placed on all sorts of objects, to show ownership or simply to add color. This jar of about 1500 has quartered arms, in which the arms of two families joined by marriage appear twice together.

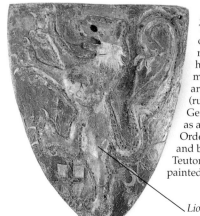

A KNIGHT'S SHIELD
This rare surviving shield of the 13th century is made from wood, which has a lion rampant moulded in leather. These are the arms of a landgrave (ruler) of Hesse in Germany. He is represented as a knight of the Teutonic Order, as the white shield and black cross of the Teutonic knights has been painted on the lower left.

Lion rampant

Arms of Cosimo de' Medici

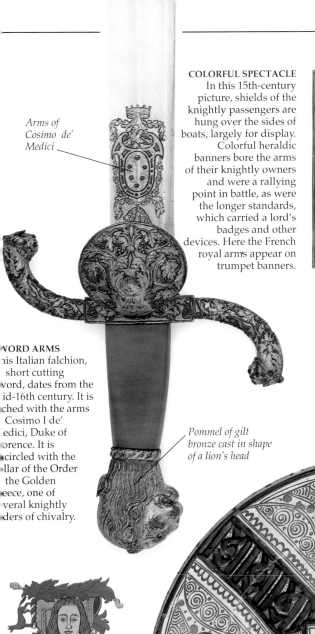

WORD ARMS
his Italian falchion, short cutting word, dates from the id-16th century. It is ched with the arms Cosimo I de' edici, Duke of orence. It is circled with the llar of the Order the Golden eece, one of veral knightly ders of chivalry.

Pommel of gilt bronze cast in shape of a lion's head

COLORFUL SPECTACLE
In this 15th-century picture, shields of the knightly passengers are hung over the sides of boats, largely for display. Colorful heraldic banners bore the arms of their knightly owners and were a rallying point in battle, as were the longer standards, which carried a lord's badges and other devices. Here the French royal arms appear on trumpet banners.

MAKING AN IMPRESSION
The bezel of this large gold 14th-century signet ring is engraved with heraldic arms, which include those of the de Grailly family. Above are the letters: "EID Gre," probably meaning: "This is the seal of Jean de Grailly." When pressed into hot wax used to seal a document, the arms appeared in the wax the right way around.

COAT OF ARMS
The brass of Sir Thomas enerhasset (died 1531) shows he heraldic arms on his coat rmor, the name given to the urcoat. The version worn at this time is the tabard, also used by heralds.

SPANISH PLATE
The Spanish kingdom of Castile had a castle for its arms, while that of Leon used a lion. These are the earliest "quartered arms," first noted in 1272. On this Spanish dish of about 1425 the true heraldic colors have been ignored, while the background has designs influenced by the Spanish Muslims.

Gules, a lion rampant or

Or, a lion sejant regardant purpure

Gules, a swan argent

Azure, a dolphin naiant argent

Or, a dragon rampant vert

Or, a portcullis purpure

Azure, a sun in splendor or

KEY TO LABELS ON ARMS	
Or	Gold
Argent	Silver
Gules	Red
Azure	Blue
Sable	Black
Vert	Green
Purpure	Purple

Hunting and hawking

Mᴇᴅɪᴇᴠᴀʟ ᴍᴏɴᴀʀᴄʜs ᴀɴᴅ ʟᴏʀᴅs were very fond of hunting and hawking. These sports provided fresh meat, as well as helped to train knights for war. Hunting, for example, allowed them to show their courage when facing dangerous animals like a wild boar. The Norman kings set aside vast areas of woodland for hunting in England, and there were severe penalties for poachers or anyone who broke the forest laws. The animals hunted ranged from deer and boar to birds and rabbits. Knights often hunted on horseback, which provided excitement and useful practice for war. Sometimes "beaters" drove the prey toward the huntsmen, who lay in wait. Hunters might also use bows or crossbows, which gave them good experience with these weapons. Hawking was very popular, and good birds were prized. One 15th-century manuscript gives a list of hawks, showing how only the higher members of society could fly the best birds.

FLYING TO A LURᴇ
A lure was a dummy bird which the falconer swung from a long cord. The falcon would pounce on the lure, so that the falconer could retrieve his bird. The lure could also be used to exercise a bird or teach it to climb high and "stoop" – dive – down onto its prey

Steel pin to engage rack for drawing bow

NOBLE BEASTS
This detail of the carving on the side of the crossbow tiller shows a stag hunt. Only rich people were allowed to hunt stags.

Wooden tiller veneered with polished stag horn carved in relief

Wooden flights

WOODEN FEATHERS
These German crossbow bolts date to about 1470. One has wooden flights rather than the feathers usually seen on arrows.

FOR DEER HUNTERS *below*
The blade of a German hunting sword of about 1540 is etched with scenes of a stag hunt. Such swords were carried for hunting and also for general protection.

WOLF HUNT
When hunting for wolves, huntsmen would hang pieces of meat in a thicket and drag them along pathways to leave a scent. Look-outs in trees warned of the wolf's approach and mastiff dogs flushed it out for the hunters. This hunt is pictured in a copy of the late-14th-century hunting book of Gaston Phoebus, Count of Foix, France.

FREDERICK II THE FALCONER
This German emperor liked falconry so much that in the mid-13th century he wrote a book on the subject, from which this picture comes. Some lords even kept hawks in their private rooms.

Deer being driven into nets

Dogs chasing the deer

Hunting horn

Man shooting squirrel

Falconer

ON THE HUNT
A Flemish or German silver plaque of about 1600 shows knights hunting with hounds, falconry, and guns. One hound catches a hare in front of three ladies who watch with interest from their carriage.

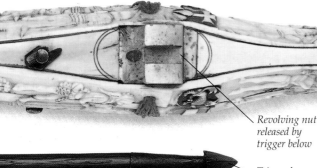

Revolving nut released by trigger below

Triangular barbed head

PET CARE
Hunting dogs needed careful looking after. Gaston Phoebus recommends the use of herbal medicines to cure mange, diseases of the eye, ear, and throat, and even rabies. Swollen paws damaged by spiny plants required attention. Dislocated shoulders were treated by bonesetters, and broken legs were put in harnesses.

AFTER THEM!
Upper-class women were also avid hunters. In this illustration of about 1340 a lady blows a hunting horn as she gallops after the dogs.

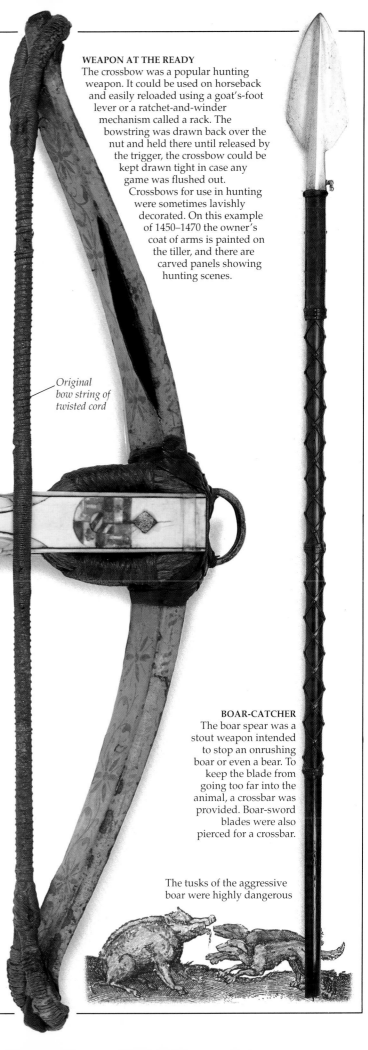

WEAPON AT THE READY
The crossbow was a popular hunting weapon. It could be used on horseback and easily reloaded using a goat's-foot lever or a ratchet-and-winder mechanism called a rack. The bowstring was drawn back over the nut and held there until released by the trigger, the crossbow could be kept drawn tight in case any game was flushed out.

Crossbows for use in hunting were sometimes lavishly decorated. On this example of 1450–1470 the owner's coat of arms is painted on the tiller, and there are carved panels showing hunting scenes.

Original bow string of twisted cord

BOAR-CATCHER
The boar spear was a stout weapon intended to stop an onrushing boar or even a bear. To keep the blade from going too far into the animal, a crossbar was provided. Boar-sword blades were also pierced for a crossbar.

The tusks of the aggressive boar were highly dangerous

The castle at war

CASTLES WERE BUILT as defense against enemy attacks. The first obstacle for the enemy was a ditch all the way around the castle, which was sometimes filled with stakes to slow a man down and make him an easy target. Moats – ditches that were often filled with water – were less common: they kept attackers from mining (burrowing) under the walls. Towers jutted out from the walls so that defending archers could shoot along the walls to repel any attackers. Small gates allowed the defenders to rush out and surprise the enemy. The castle was also used as a base from which knights rode out to fight an enemy or ravage his lands.

Iron-clad wooden portcullis

Wooden doors barred from behind

GATEHOUSE
The gatehouse was always strongly defended, as it was thought to be a weak spot. Usually a wooden lifting bridge spanned the ditch and an iron gate called portcullis could be lowered to form a barrier

VAULTED CEILING
There are holes built into the stone vaulted ceiling of the castle gatehouse. These allowed people on the floor above to pour water down to put out fires, or possibly to drop stones or boiling water onto the heads of attackers.

High turrets gave clear views of approaching enemies

Gap (or crenel), through which defenders could shoot

Merlon to protect defenders against missiles

Round flanking tower; the shape leaves no corners for a battering ram or miners

Machicolations along gate tower

Battlement on section of curtain wall

OVER THE WALLS

This early 14th-century picture shows the 11th-century Crusader Godfrey of Bouillon attacking fortifications. His men are using scaling ladders, which was always dangerous because the defenders would try to push them away. Archers provide covering fire.

EMBRASURE

An embrasure was an alcove in the thickness of the wall, with a narrow opening, or "loophole," to the outside. This allowed defenders to look and shoot out without showing themselves. In this example, the rounded lower part of the loophole is designed for guns, used more and more in warfare by the time this castle was built.

FLANKING TOWERS

This picture was taken looking up the front of the castle. Flanking towers jut out on either side to protect the gate. The battlements are thrust forward (machicolated) so that they overhang the walls. Boiling water or hot sand could be poured through the holes to hurt the attackers below. The holes could also be used to pour cold water, to put out fires.

Stone corbel supports the battlement

AT SIEGE

Both the attackers and the defenders of this castle are using siege engines to hurl missiles at each other.

KNIGHTLY STRONGHOLD

Bodiam Castle in Sussex, England, was built in 1385 by Sir Edward Dalyngrigge amid fears of a French invasion. It has a single stone curtain wall with round towers at the corners and is surrounded by a broad moat to protect the occupants. To guard against possible treachery among the defending soldiers, there are no connecting doors between their quarters and those of the lord.

Turret or watchtower

Lancet window to let in light but keep out missiles

Laying a siege

IF SURROUNDING a castle and trying to starve the defenders into submission did not work, attackers could try to take it by force. They could tunnel under the walls to topple them, or come up inside the courtyard. Defenders might place bowls of water on the ground so that any tunneling activity made the water ripple. Then they could dig countermines to break into the tunnels, leading to a fierce struggle underground. Attackers might also try to break down the walls using artillery or battering rams slung under movable sheds. Defenders lowered hooks to catch the heads of battering rams, or dropped mattresses to cushion the blows. A direct assault over the walls meant using scaling ladders to hook onto battlements; this was dangerous as defenders pushed them away from the walls with forked poles.

CHIPPING AWAY
Under cover of a shed on wheels, miners pick away stones at the wall base. Wooden props were then inserted and burned to make the wall collapse.

Wheel to move shield

MOVABLE SHIELD
Archers and crossbowmen used these shields to protect themselves while trying to pick off defenders and covering assaults.

Sling

MOUTHPIECE
From the 12th century, heralds were used to demand surrender on their lord's behalf. They wore the lord's coat of arms for recognition.

Pivoting arm

Counterweight

Large stones for use as missiles

PEOPLE POWER
The traction trebuchet, which probably appeared in the mid-12th century, had a team of men hauling on ropes at the short end of a beam, so pivoting up the other end with its sling. This opened to release a large stone.

Ropes for hauling

HEAVYWEIGHT
The counterpoise trebuchet, which probably appeared in the late 12th century, used a huge box of earth and stones instead of manpower to pull down the arm and send a missile flying into the air.

Winch

KEEP YOUR HEAD UP
Severed enemy heads were sometimes thrown to demoralize the opposition. Messengers with rejected terms might be trussed up in a trebuchet, or dung or dead animals thrown to spread disease.

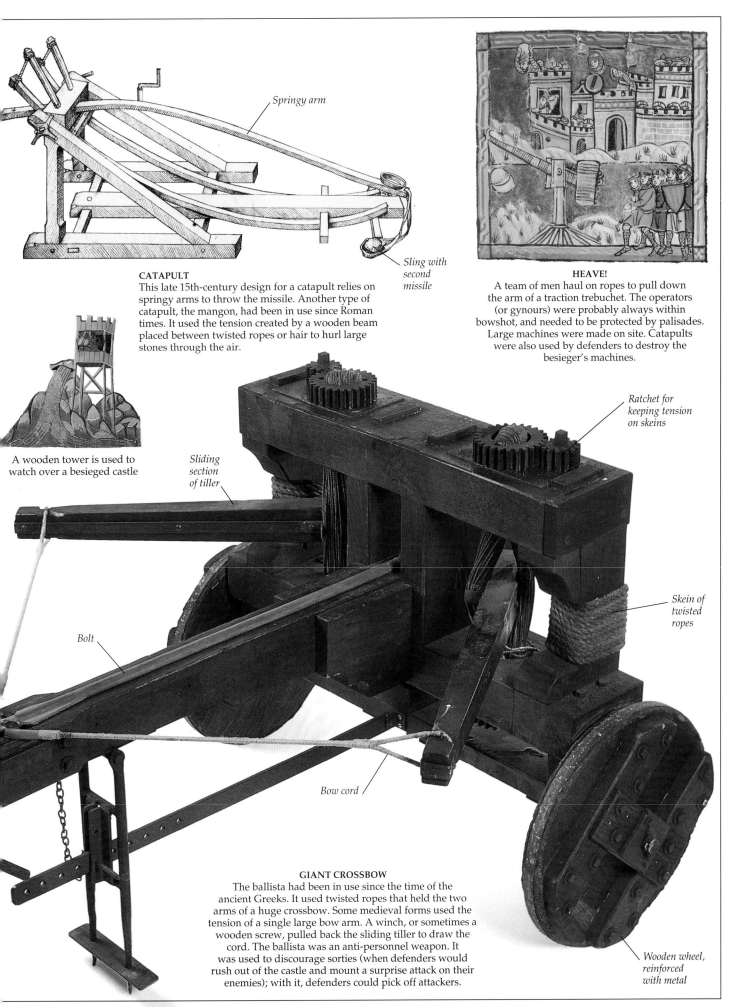

CATAPULT

This late 15th-century design for a catapult relies on springy arms to throw the missile. Another type of catapult, the mangon, had been in use since Roman times. It used the tension created by a wooden beam placed between twisted ropes or hair to hurl large stones through the air.

Springy arm

Sling with second missile

HEAVE!

A team of men haul on ropes to pull down the arm of a traction trebuchet. The operators (or gynours) were probably always within bowshot, and needed to be protected by palisades. Large machines were made on site. Catapults were also used by defenders to destroy the besieger's machines.

A wooden tower is used to watch over a besieged castle

Sliding section of tiller

Ratchet for keeping tension on skeins

Skein of twisted ropes

Bolt

Bow cord

GIANT CROSSBOW

The ballista had been in use since the time of the ancient Greeks. It used twisted ropes that held the two arms of a huge crossbow. Some medieval forms used the tension of a single large bow arm. A winch, or sometimes a wooden screw, pulled back the sliding tiller to draw the cord. The ballista was an anti-personnel weapon. It was used to discourage sorties (when defenders would rush out of the castle and mount a surprise attack on their enemies); with it, defenders could pick off attackers.

Wooden wheel, reinforced with metal

Tricks of defense

THE FIRST OBSTACLE faced by someone attacking a castle was a wet or dry moat. A moat made it difficult for attackers to bring siege machines near the castle. If dry, stakes might be planted to slow an enemy and make him an easier target. The gatehouse was an obvious weak spot, so a *barbican*, or defensive work, was sometimes placed in front to guard the approach. A drawbridge and portcullis gave extra protection. The portcullis was an iron-covered wooden grille moving up and down in slots on either side of the entrance passage. It was raised by a winch in a room above and could be dropped quickly if danger threatened. Drawbridges over the ditch took several forms, including simple wooden platforms which were pulled back, lifting bridges attached by chains to pulleys, and turning bridges pivoted like a seesaw.

DROPPING IN
The gate passage at Bodiam has so-called "murder holes" (*meutrières*) in the roof so cold water could be poured down to put out fires. Also scalding water, hot sand, or other offensive substances might be dropped on enemies who managed to get in.

GATEHOUSE
This castle's passage is flanked by huge towers. Missiles could be dropped on an attacker through slots over the arch.

FLARING BASE
The Castel Nuovo ("new castle") in Naples, Italy, has a *chemise*, or small outer wall. This wall has a splayed-out base (called a batter or talus), so that missiles dropped from above bounce out toward the enemy. It also thickened the wall, giving added protection against attacks by battering rams, undermining, or bombardment. The castle was rebuilt in the years 1442-1458 as an early experiment against artillery, so this example was also designed to deflect enemy cannon balls.

Curtain wall

Corbel supporting machicolated parapet

Batter or talus

MACHICOLATIONS

Machicolations were stone versions of wooden hoardings and developed in the 12th century. The battlements jutted beyond the walls and were supported on stone corbels. Gaps left between the corbels allowed offensive material to be dropped on enemies at the wall base.

GUN-PORT
In the late 14th century keyhole-shaped gun-ports appeared. Round ports were usually for handguns while horizontal slots were for small cannon mounted behind walls. This example is from the Pfalzgrafenstein in Germany.

STICKING OUT
The Pfalzgrafenstein on the Rhine has a number of hoardings built out from the tops of its walls. These are wooden constructions with gaps in the floor allowing defenders to drop missiles on attackers at the foot of the wall without having to expose themselves by leaning out over the battlements. Hot water, red-hot sand, or rocks might be thrown, as well as quicklime. Boiling oil, beloved of film-makers, is rarely mentioned.

Steep roof to throw off missiles

Slots for observation and shooting through

Wooden walls

Timber support

LIFTING BRIDGES
The *bascule* bridge had chains attached to wooden beams weighted at the rear. This end dropped when released, lifting the front of the bridge into recesses in the wall.

Manuscript showing lifting bridge with wooden beams and chains

Pedestrian and main lifting bridges at Langeais, France

Machicolated parapet

Turret for observation

CURTAINS AND FLANKS
The 14th-century castle at Bodiam, England, has stretches of curtain walls protected by flanking towers which jut out beyond the wall face.

Round tower, less vulnerable to miners than sharp angles

Loophole

The garrison

Basinet

Mail curtain
(or aventail)

Steel
gauntlet

Jupon

THE BODY OF SOLDIERS who lived in a castle and
defended it was called the garrison. In early castles,
especially at times of unrest, these men might be
knights who lived permanently in their lord's castle.
In return for accommodation they fought for the
lord and guarded the castle. Gradually more knights
settled on their own estates, and the knightly duties
were done using a rotation system. A knight stayed
in the castle for a set period, then he was replaced
by another man. During the 14th and 15th centuries
it became more common for hired soldiers to
guard castles, although this tended to increase
the fear of betrayal.

Part of
shield

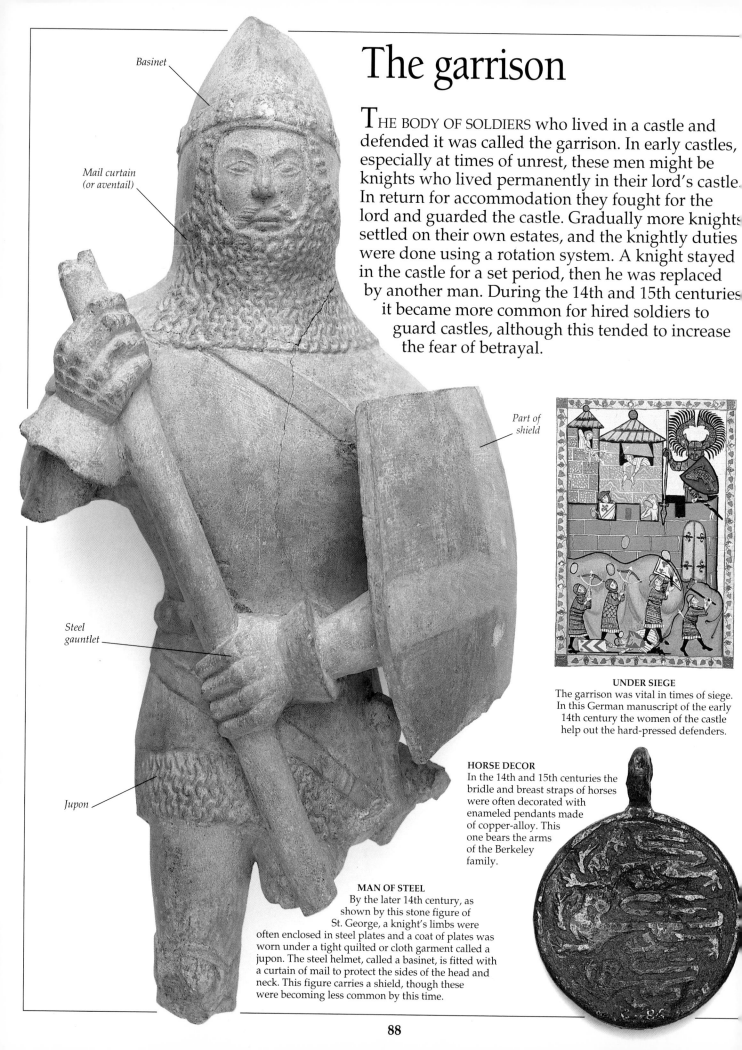

UNDER SIEGE
The garrison was vital in times of siege.
In this German manuscript of the early
14th century the women of the castle
help out the hard-pressed defenders.

HORSE DECOR
In the 14th and 15th centuries the
bridle and breast straps of horses
were often decorated with
enameled pendants made
of copper-alloy. This
one bears the arms
of the Berkeley
family.

MAN OF STEEL
By the later 14th century, as
shown by this stone figure of
St. George, a knight's limbs were
often enclosed in steel plates and a coat of plates was
worn under a tight quilted or cloth garment called a
jupon. The steel helmet, called a basinet, is fitted with
a curtain of mail to protect the sides of the head and
neck. This figure carries a shield, though these
were becoming less common by this time.

KNIGHTLY DUTIES
Castles usually had only a small garrison in peacetime, and even in times of trouble soldiers were usually counted in tens rather than in hundreds. The garrison provided a ready supply of knights, men-at-arms, and squires when a lord needed them. Armed men were needed not only in time of war. Lords used armed men as escorts to protect them on the roads, especially from robbers in wooded areas. In this 14th-century picture the arrival of armored men is greeted by fanfares from the castle.

Loop for chain

Dragon emblem

Arms of Cresci family

Worn white enamel decoration

DRAGON
This badge dates from the 15th century and depicts a dragon. This creature was a common emblem in heraldry. The badge is decorated with enamel, and was worn as a pendant.

Modern mount

Bishop's miter

Wild boar

Round-topped shield, typically Italian in shape

MEDALLION
This silver medallion comes from Florence, Italy, and dates from the 14th century. The right-hand shield may show the arms of the Cresci family, suggesting that it could have belonged to one of that family's retainers.

OLD BOAR
This 15th-century horse pendant was, like the others, cast in copper-alloy and decorated with enamel. The decoration shows a wild boar and a bishop's miter. The pendant has been cut down and mounted.

MULBERRY BUSH
This badge of a mulberry bush belonged to a retainer of the Mowbray family. Followers of noble families often wore metal badges like this, or cloth badges stitched to their clothing for identification.

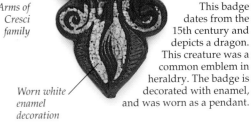

FIGHTING MAN
Knights who garrisoned Norman castles had coats of mail, steel helmets, and large wooden shields.

THORN IN THE SIDE
Castles were not just fortified dwellings. They were bases from which soldiers controlled the surrounding countryside. This meant that an invader of an area first had to attack the local castles, or run the risk of his supply lines being cut.

Mail gusset

Arming doublet

Arming for the fight

EARLY ARMOR was quite easy to put on. Mail was pulled on over the head, and a coat of plates (pp. 60-61) was buckled at the back, or at the sides and shoulders. Plate armor was more tricky to put on, but a knight could be armed by his squire in a few minutes and the armor could be speedily removed if necessary. After putting on a garment called an arming doublet, a knight was always armed form the feet upward, finishing with the helmet. In the 15th century, certain pieces of armor were laced to the arming doublet, but in the following century these pieces were more often attached to each other by straps or rivets. Here a squire is arming a knight in late-15th-century German "Gothic" style armor.

Waxed points

1 ARMING DOUBLET
This padded garment has waxed thongs (called points) to fasten different parts of the armor. Therefore the armor cannot be put on without the arming doublet. The mail gussets on the doublet are under the gaps that will be left by the plates.

Cuisse
Poleyn
Greave
Sabaton

2 SABATON, GREAVE, POLEYN, AND CUISSE
The sabaton and greave, for foot and lower leg, are followed by the poleyn, which is attached to the cuisse. The top edge is laced up to the torso.

Backplate
Flanged edge
Breast-plate
Waist strap

3 MAIL SKIRT
Mail is secured around the waist to protect the groin, another area not fully covered by the plates. Using flexible mail here makes it easier to bend or sit.

4 BACKPLATE
The backplate is placed in position. It has a flanged lower edge to deflect weapons from the buttocks and legs. A strap and buckle are riveted to the lower front edges.

5 BREASTPLATE
Breast and back together are called the cuirass. They are held together by the waist straps and are also connected at the shoulders.

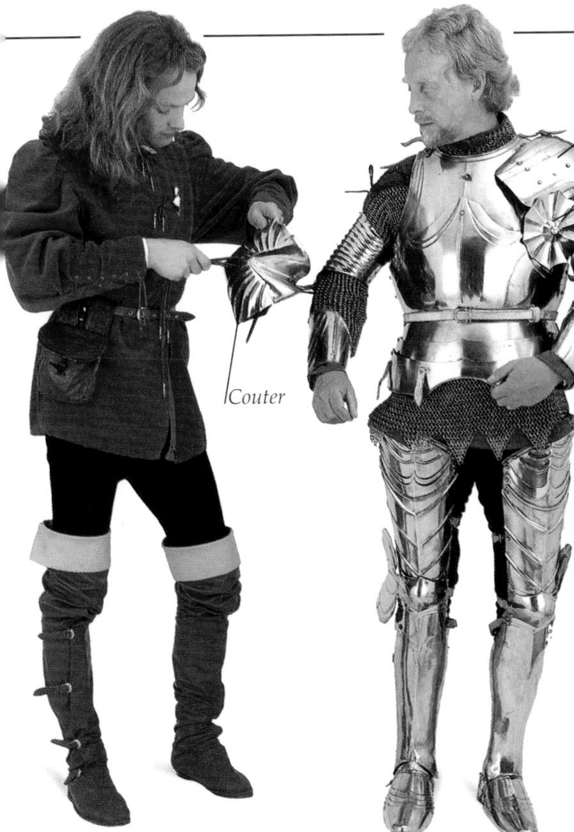

Pauldron

Besague

Vambrace

Vambrace

Couter

Leather
glove inside
gauntlet

Rondel
dagger

Sword belt

Sword

7 GAUNTLETS, SWORD, AND DAGGER

The gauntlets are fitted with a leather glove to allow the knight to grip his weapons. His sword belt has straps to hold the scabbard at a convenient angle. A rondel dagger hangs at his right side.

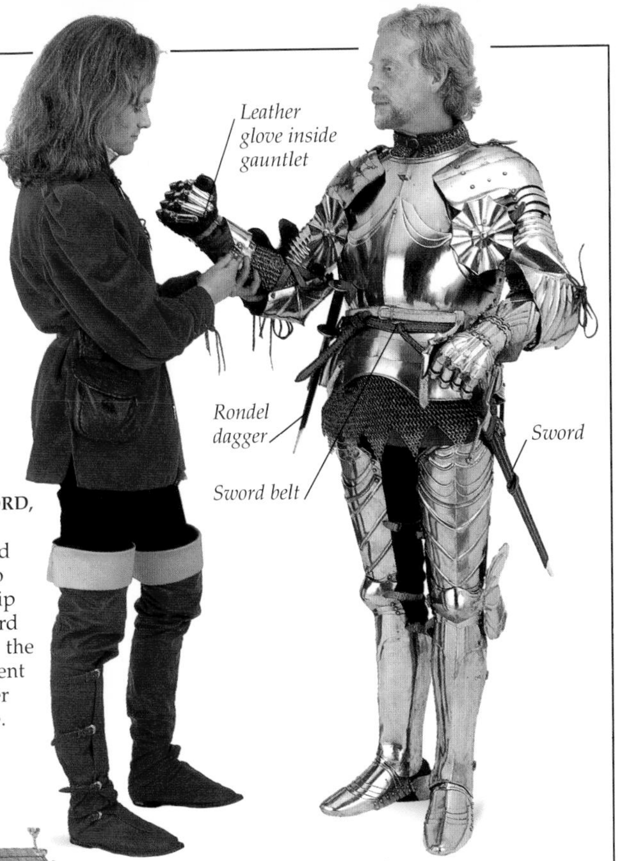

6 PAULDRON, COUTER, VAMBRACE, AND BESAGUE

The upper arm guard (vambrace) and elbow piece (couter) are tied by laces through pairs of holes in the plates. The pauldron and besague guard the knight's shoulder and armpit.

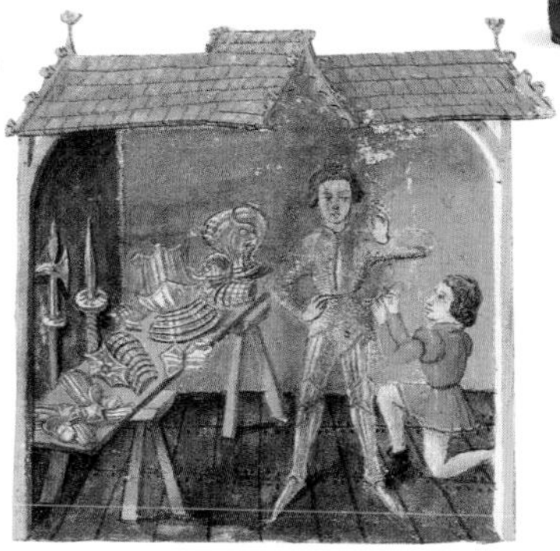

ARMING A KNIGHT

A rare picture of about 1450 shows a knight being armed for foot combat in the lists. His arming doublet can be seen.

10 FULLY ARMED

The knight holds a mace, which is an effective weapon against plate armor. Armed from head to foot (or cap-a-pie) he is now ready to mount his warhorse.

Bevor

Helmet

Mace

Rowel
spur

8 BEVOR

A "bevor," or chin defense, is added to protect the lower half of the face when wearing the sallet, a form of helmet especially popular in Germany.

9 SPURS AND HELMET

The knight's rowel spurs (pp. 68-69) are buckled to his feet; the helmet, lined inside for comfort and to cushion blows, is placed on his head. The helmet has a chin strap to keep it from being knocked off in combat.

The enemy

KNIGHTS SOON FOUND THEMSELVES facing infantry capable of defeating them. The English axmen at Hastings in 1066 cut down Norman knights, while Flemish footsoldiers with clubs defeated French horsemen at Courtrai in 1302. Massed Scottish spear formations stopped cavalry charges at Bannockburn in 1314. The Swiss favored the same tactic but used pikes. Different types of bow were highly effective against mounted knights. English longbowmen broke up cavalry charges by French knights at Crécy in 1346 and dismounted knights at Agincourt in 1415. The lethal crossbow shot short bolts from increasingly powerful weapons. In 15th-century Bohemia (now part of the Czech lands) the Hussites blasted German knights, using the first massed guns, fired from the protection of wagons.

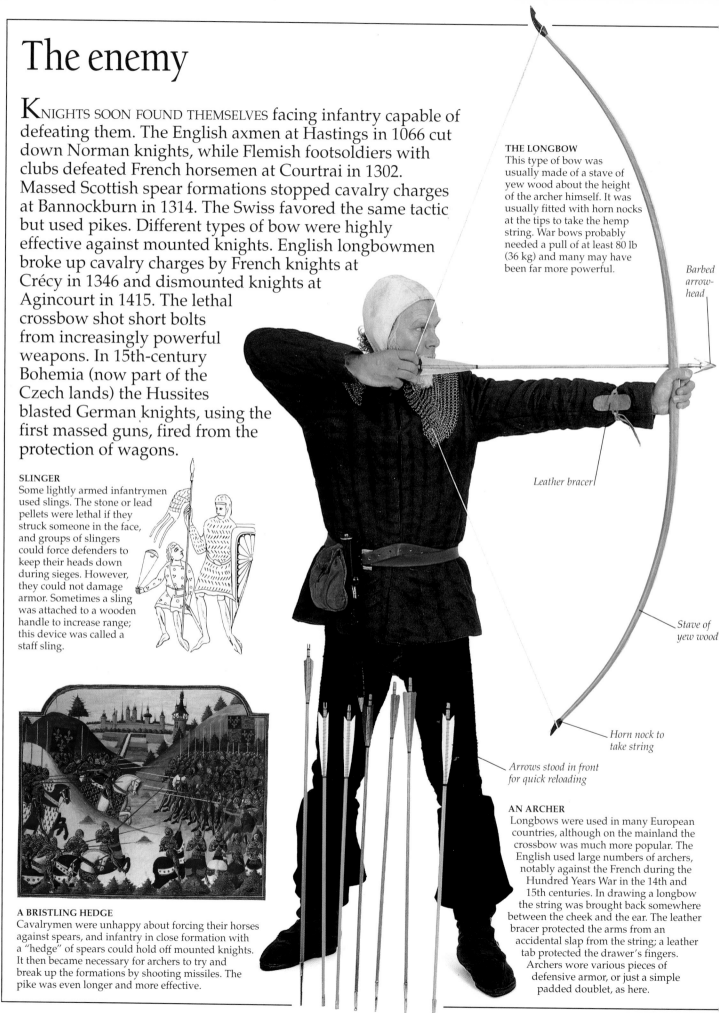

SLINGER
Some lightly armed infantrymen used slings. The stone or lead pellets were lethal if they struck someone in the face, and groups of slingers could force defenders to keep their heads down during sieges. However, they could not damage armor. Sometimes a sling was attached to a wooden handle to increase range; this device was called a staff sling.

THE LONGBOW
This type of bow was usually made of a stave of yew wood about the height of the archer himself. It was usually fitted with horn nocks at the tips to take the hemp string. War bows probably needed a pull of at least 80 lb (36 kg) and many may have been far more powerful.

Barbed arrow-head

Leather bracer

Stave of yew wood

Horn nock to take string

Arrows stood in front for quick reloading

A BRISTLING HEDGE
Cavalrymen were unhappy about forcing their horses against spears, and infantry in close formation with a "hedge" of spears could hold off mounted knights. It then became necessary for archers to try and break up the formations by shooting missiles. The pike was even longer and more effective.

AN ARCHER
Longbows were used in many European countries, although on the mainland the crossbow was much more popular. The English used large numbers of archers, notably against the French during the Hundred Years War in the 14th and 15th centuries. In drawing a longbow the string was brought back somewhere between the cheek and the ear. The leather bracer protected the arms from an accidental slap from the string; a leather tab protected the drawer's fingers. Archers wore various pieces of defensive armor, or just a simple padded doublet, as here.

AT THE BUTTS

The strength required to pull a longbow meant that archers needed constant practice to keep in condition and maintain their skills. In this 14th-century picture English archers shoot at the butts, targets set up on earthen mounds.

THE GOOSE FEATHER

Fletchings, or feather flights, make the arrow spin for a truer flight. Usually goose feathers were used for the vast numbers of arrows needed by an army. The shaft was commonly made from ash wood. The nock holds the arrow lightly on the string.

Nock inset into shaft *Goose feather* *Binding*

Fragment of shaft

General-purpose

Bodkin   Bodkin

General-purpose   Broadhead

ARROWHEADS

These varied in shape depending on their use. Broadheads were barbed for use against animals; some were used against warhorses. Bodkins were for penetrating armor. A thin bodkin could pierce armor plate when it struck its target squarely. There were also general-purpose arrowheads.

LONG-RANGE FIGHTING

Arrows from a longbow could probably fly about 1,000 ft (300 m), which meant that a "creeping barrage" of arrows could be dropped on an advancing enemy. This was done by shooting the arrows upward. Cavalry horses were especially vulnerable – some part of the horse was always unprotected and became uncontrollable when wounded. Bodkins could punch through mail links.

Bodkin

Steel buckler or fist shield

Arrow through belt

Pieces of leg armor for partial protection

WELSH ARCHER

The English came up against Welsh longbowmen in the 12th century, and such men were often employed in English armies afterward. In this crude picture the rough bow is shown far too small. The bare foot may be to give a better grip.

LONGBOW VERSUS CROSSBOW

A skilled archer might release 12 arrows per minute. A crossbowman, using a windlass (mechanical winder), could only shoot two bolts in the same time. But these would penetrate deeply, and the crossbowman did not need so much training. In this late-15th-century illustration the crossbowman uses a windlass to pull back a powerful steel bow arm.

KEEN EYE

Each archer carried 24 arrows, known as a sheaf, and when these were shot away more were brought from supply wagons. Many archers carried their arrows pushed through their belt rather than in a quiver, which was also usually hung from the waist. They would often stick their arrows into the ground in front of them, ready for quick shooting.

Into battle

THE RULES OF CHIVALRY dictated that knights should show courtesy to defeated enemies. This was not just humane, it brought ransoms from high-ranking prisoners. But this code was not always observed, especially by desperate men facing death. For example, English longbowmen supported by knights slaughtered French knights at the battles of Crécy (1346), Poitiers (1356), and Agincourt (1415). And knights often showed little mercy to foot soldiers, cutting them down ruthlessly in pursuit. Much was at stake in a battle; defeat might mean the loss of an army or even a throne. So commanders preferred to ravage and raid enemy territory. This brought extra supplies as well as destroying property, and showed that the local lord could not protect his people in turn. Keeping troops close to an enemy's army kept it from ravaging in turn.

WARRIOR KINGS
The great seals of many medieval kings showed them as head of their army, on horseback, and wearing full armor. Nobles also liked to portray themselves in this way. Here Henry I, king of England (1100–1135) and duke of Normandy, wears a mail coat and conical helmet.

FIGHTING ON FOOT
Although knights were trained as horsemen, they did not always go into battle as cavalrymen. On many occasions it was thought better for a large part of an army to dismount and form a solid body, often supported by archers and groups of cavalry. In this late-14th century illustration, dismounted English and French knights and men-at-arms, many wearing visored basinets on their heads (pp. 60-61), clash on a bridge. Archers and crossbowmen assist them.

CALTROPS
These nasty-looking iron objects are only a couple of inches high. They were scattered over the ground before a battle to lame horses or men from the opposing army who accidentally stepped on them. However they fell, caltrops always landed with one spike pointing upward. They were also scattered in front of castles.

IN PURSUIT
A mid-13th-century battle scene shows the point when one force in the battle has turned in flight and is pursued by the other side. Often the pursuers did not hesitate to strike at men with their backs turned, and once a man was down, his opponent would give him several further cuts to make sure he stayed there. Breaking ranks to chase the enemy could sometimes put the rest of your army in danger.

WALL OF HORSES *above*
Armor of the 12th century was similar in many parts of Europe, but fighting methods could vary. Instead of using their lances to stab overhand or even to throw, as sometimes happened in the 11th century, the Italian knights on this stone carving are "couching" – tucking – them under their arms. Each side charges in close formation, hoping to steamroller over their opponents.

One spike always points upward

SHOCK OF BATTLE
This late-15th-century picture shows the crash of two opposing cavalry forces in full plate armor and the deadly effects of well-aimed lances. Those struck down in the first line, even if only slightly wounded, were liable to be trampled by the horses either of the enemy or of their own knights following behind.

SPOILS OF WAR
When an army was defeated the victors would often capture the baggage. This could contain many valuables, especially if the losing leader was a prince. Captured towns also provided rich pickings, and prisoners and dead knights were stripped of their armor after a battle. In this 14th-century Italian picture the victors examine the spoils.

SHOCK WAVES
This early-16th-century German woodcut shows a disciplined charge by mounted knights. Spurring their horses to a gallop as they near the enemy, the first line has made contact while those behind follow with lances still raised. They will lower their lances before meeting their opponents.

Three spikes rest on the ground

The chapel

The dead were wrapped in cloth shrouds. A coffin was often used to take a dead body to the grave.

THE CHAPEL WAS an important room in a Christian castle, because inhabitants were expected to join in regular services. In early towers the chapel was often on the top floor or in an upper room in the entrance building. As castles developed, the chapel became part of the domestic range of buildings. It might be decorated with carved stonework and wall paintings that often illustrated a Bible story, because few people could read the Bible itself and so many relied on pictures. The clergy were among the few who could read and write and so, in addition to their religious duties, they looked after the documents relating to the castle. A chaplain therefore often had several clerks to help him.

FAITH AND POLITICS
This 15th-century illustration shows Thomas Arundel, archbishop of Canterbury, England, preaching the cause of Henry IV. Banished by Richard II, Henry IV landed in England in 1399 with Thomas and, supported by a group of nobles, seized the crown. Medieval churchmen were often mixed up with political intrigues. Bishops did not work in castle chapels; the most powerful of them held castles in their own right.

ROYAL CUP
The Royal Gold Cup was made in about 1380 for the Duke of Berry in France and has been in the possession of both English and French kings. It is decorated in colored enamels with scenes of saints' lives – religious teaching was always present in every medieval household.

Scene of the adoration of the Magi

Magi awakened by an angel

TEACHING IN STONE
The entrance to the chapel at the castle of Loches in France dates from the late 12th century. The doorway is carved with figures which were designed to help teach people who were unable to read.

Statue of a bishop

Saint Peter

Carvings of animals and mythical beasts

Holy water stoup

96

Sword with broad,
diamond-sectioned blade

Gauntlet

Priest
attending
Becket

This miter (bishop's hat)
was probably Becket's

SEAL
Becket's seal shows an
early miter worn side-on.
Later bishops, like
Thomas Arundel on the
opposite page, wore their
miters front-on, as
bishops do today.

Thomas
Becket in
prayer at
the altar

Poleyn

MARTYRDOM
This piece of alabaster
is carved with a scene
of the death of Thomas
Becket in 1170, though the
knights all wear armor of
the late 14th century,
when the carving was
made. Becket
was archbishop of
Canterbury under Henry
II of England, but the two
men constantly argued.
After an angry outburst
by Henry, four knights
murdered Becket in
his own cathedral.
He was soon hailed as
a saint and Canterbury
became a great shrine
for pilgrims.

Holy orders

"WE MUST FORM A SCHOOL IN THE LORD'S SERVICE," wrote St. Benedict in the sixth century. He founded a monastery at Monte Cassino in Italy where monks could live, work, and pray together. The monks became known as the Benedictines because they followed St. Benedict's "Rule," which instructed them to make three vows – of poverty (to own no property), chastity (never to marry), and obedience (to obey the orders of their leaders). Making these vows was a serious undertaking, so St. Benedict ordered that every novice, or newcomer, should live in the monastery for a year before committing himself. Once he had made his vows, a novice had the crown of his head shaved in a tonsure and became a brother of the order. In time, monasteries and convents throughout Europe adopted St. Benedict's Rule.

12th-century Celtic monk

Tonsure

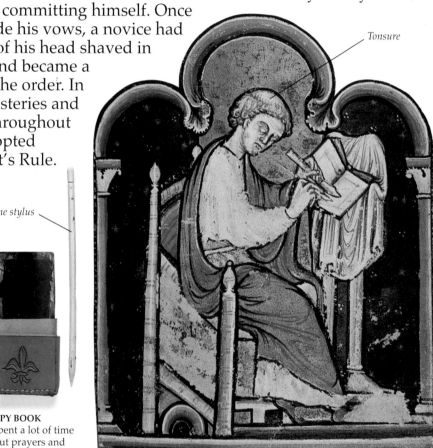

Bone stylus

Wax tablet on a horn base

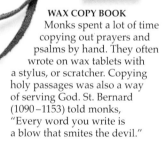

WAX COPY BOOK
Monks spent a lot of time copying out prayers and psalms by hand. They often wrote on wax tablets with a stylus, or scratcher. Copying holy passages was also a way of serving God. St. Bernard (1090–1153) told monks, "Every word you write is a blow that smites the devil."

THE HISTORY MAN
Many monks were well educated, and monasteries became centers of learning. St. Bede (c. 673–735), also known as the Venerable Bede, was an English Benedictine monk who devoted his life to writing and scholarship. He wrote books on science, religion, and history, including the great *Ecclesiastical History of the English Nation*. Without monks like Bede, we would know much less about the history of the Middle Ages.

NO LIGHT IN THE DARKNESS
St. Benedict's Rule allowed for basic comforts, but life in a monastery was never easy. At first, monks were not allowed candles for reading at services – they had to learn all the prayers, psalms, and other forms of worship by heart.

OUT OF ORDER
By the tenth century, many religious houses had become too relaxed. The monk below has been placed in the stocks with his mistress as a punishment for an illicit affair. Some French monks thought that the ideals of St. Benedict were being forgotten and formed a new order at Cluny in 910. The Cluniacs tried to follow the strict and simple rule laid down by St. Benedict. Other new orders were the Carthusians, who believed in a life of silent prayer, and the Cistercians, who thought that hard work was the best way to serve God.

THE FRANCISCANS
St. Francis of Assisi (c. 1182–1226) was the son of a rich man, yet he gave away all his possessions to live like one of Christ's disciples. He founded a new order of holy brothers in Italy called Franciscan friars. Instead of living in monasteries, they took the word of God to the people, traveling about preaching and begging for their food. An order of Franciscan nuns was founded by St. Clare, one of St. Francis's followers.

Plain rope belt

Bare feet

HEAD WARMER
In winter, chilly drafts whistled through the stone corridors and bare cells of a monastery. Only the sickroom was always heated. Although the monastic way of life was often harsh, St. Benedict did not believe that monks should sacrifice their health in the service of God. His Rule stated that a monk's clothes should be plain but comfortable, and Benedictines were allowed to wear linen coifs such as this one to keep their heads warm. The Cistercians rejected such soft ways. Many of them went barefoot, and some even wore hairy underclothes as a sign of their devotion to God.

Paternoster, or wooden bead rosary, for counting prayers

Linen shift worn underneath the habit

Eating knife

Warm cloak worn in cold weather

Benedictines were allowed to wear leather belts

Long woolen habit was supposed to emulate Roman clothing

Simple, hand-sewn leather shoes; Benedictines did not have to wear sandals

HABIT OF A LIFETIME
The oldest and largest of the monastic orders, the Benedictines were known as the Black Monks because of the color of their habits. Each of the new orders formed in the 10th, 11th, and 12th centuries had its own distinguishing dress. For example, the Cistercians wore rough tunics of undyed wool and became known as the White Monks. Nevertheless, the basic style of the habit has remained the same to this day.

Life in a monastery

MONASTERIES AND CONVENTS were worlds of their own. Ruled by an abbot or an abbess, they were cut off from society and governed by special rules. When a novice (p. 98) entered a holy order, he or she was expected to stay there for the rest of his or her life. From that moment on, every part of his or her day was accounted for. Much of the time was spent attending the eight daily church services and reading or copying religious texts. Other duties included caring for the poor and sick, teaching younger members of the order, or tending to the gardens, fishponds, mill, and farm. There was a general rule of silence in most religious houses, and daily tasks had to be carried out without speaking. Although they lived apart from society, monks and nuns served an important role in the community. They provided food for the poor, care for the sick, and accommodation for pilgrims and other travelers.

ROUND OF PRAYERS
Monks went to the monastery church eight times a day in an unchanging round of offices, or services. The first, Matins, began at two o'clock in the morning, and dormitories were built near the church so that the monks wouldn't be late for services. In the early 11th century, monks at Canterbury, England, had to sing 55 psalms, one after the other, without sitting down. The Benedictines shown here at least have pews to rest on.

Single-chambered wicker beehive daubed with clay

Straw "hackle," or jacket, placed over the hive in winter to keep the bees warm

Statue of Mary and Jesus

Wicker beehive made from woven willow or hazel

BUSY BEES
The Cistercians (p. 98) believed that performing hard manual labor was the best way to lead a holy life. They built large monasteries in remote rural areas where they could farm the land in peace. Their estates grew so big that lay brothers (those who had taken holy vows but lacked the education to become monks) were taken on to help. Most monasteries had to produce their own food. These skeps, or beehives, provided honey to eat and wax for candles.

Abbey church

CARE IN A CONVENT
Nuns took the same vows as monks (p. 98) and lived in much the same way. Devoted to serving the poor, most convents and monasteries ran hospitals to care for the sick. These were open to all, and nuns and monks were instructed to "receive the patients as you would Christ Himself." The medicines and treatments may have been primitive, but at least patients were given food and a clean bed. Without the work of the Church, there would have been very little health care in the Middle Ages.

Model of an abbey in the 15th century

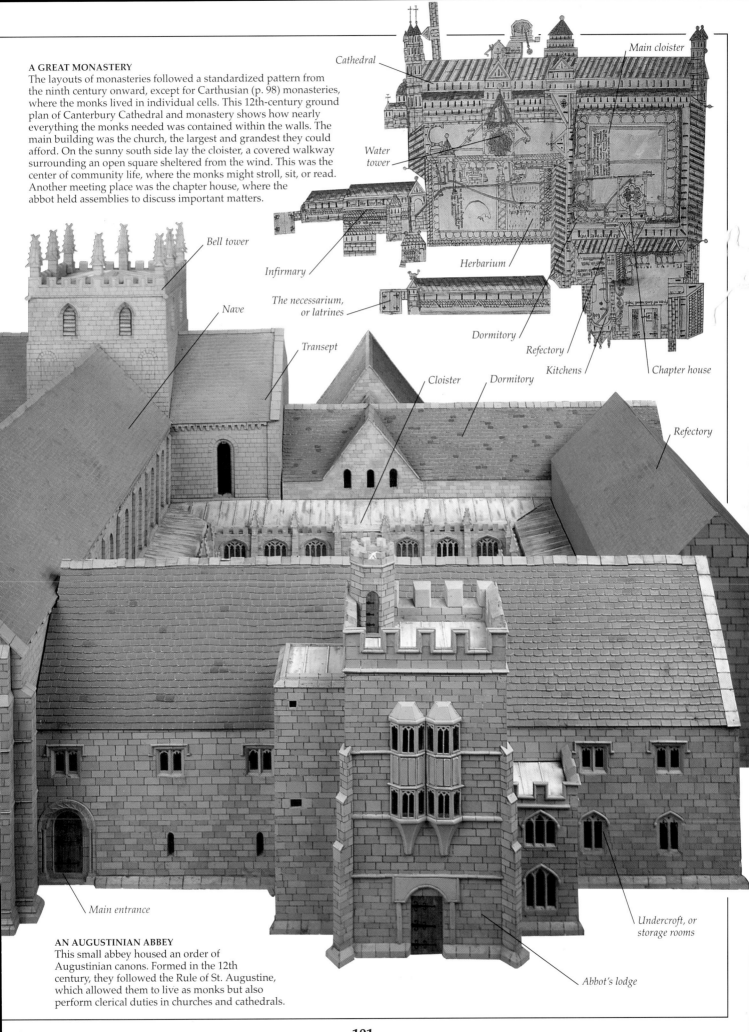

A GREAT MONASTERY

The layouts of monasteries followed a standardized pattern from the ninth century onward, except for Carthusian (p. 98) monasteries, where the monks lived in individual cells. This 12th-century ground plan of Canterbury Cathedral and monastery shows how nearly everything the monks needed was contained within the walls. The main building was the church, the largest and grandest they could afford. On the sunny south side lay the cloister, a covered walkway surrounding an open square sheltered from the wind. This was the center of community life, where the monks might stroll, sit, or read. Another meeting place was the chapter house, where the abbot held assemblies to discuss important matters.

Cathedral

Main cloister

Water tower

Infirmary

The necessarium, or latrines

Herbarium

Dormitory

Refectory

Kitchens

Chapter house

Bell tower

Nave

Transept

Cloister

Dormitory

Refectory

Main entrance

Abbot's lodge

Undercroft, or storage rooms

AN AUGUSTINIAN ABBEY

This small abbey housed an order of Augustinian canons. Formed in the 12th century, they followed the Rule of St. Augustine, which allowed them to live as monks but also perform clerical duties in churches and cathedrals.

The written word

UNTIL 1100, BOOKS WERE RARE and were usually found only in monastery libraries. Everything was written by hand, and monks spent many hours in the "scriptorium," copying out religious texts. A long manuscript such as the Bible might take one scribe a year to complete. As a way of glorifying God, many manuscripts were beautifully illuminated, or decorated, with jewel-like paints and precious gold leaf. After 1200, books became more common, especially when the first universities opened in Paris and Bologna. Professional scribes and illuminators began to produce books as well as the monks, often making copies to order for wealthy customers. Personal books of psalms, called psalters, became popular among the aristocracy.

1 GESSO WORK
One of the most striking features of medieval manuscripts are the beautifully decorated capital letters that begin each page. Painted in vibrant colors, they were often gilded with gold leaf to make them even brighter. The first stage of illuminating a letter is applying the gesso, a kind of glue made from plaster, white lead, water, sugar, and eggwhite, which makes a sticky surface for the gold leaf.

The gold leaf only sticks to the moist gesso

The molded gesso gives a 3-D effect to the gilded leaves

Each leaf is burnished separately

3 BURNISHED BRIGHT
Once the gold leaf has set into the gesso, the illuminator rubs it, or burnishes it, to make it shiny. The traditional burnishing tool was a dog's or wolf's tooth attached to a wooden handle. Finally, the rest of the background is carefully painted in around the gilding.

2 GILDING THE LETTER
The gesso is left to set over night, and the next day the illuminator smooths any rough edges and breathes on the gesso to make it slightly moist. He then lays a sheet of gold leaf over the gesso, covers it with a silk cloth, and presses it firmly onto the glue. The surplus gold is removed with a soft brush.

SCRIBES AND SCHOLARS
However hard scribes worked, books remained scarce. Few people could afford to buy them, and scholars had to travel to monastic libraries to study the texts they wanted. This statue of a scholar is from Chartres Cathedral, France.

4 SHINING THROUGH THE AGES
The finished letter is like a tiny work of art. Apart from leaves and flowers, many illuminated initials contain pictures of people and animals. If the gold is properly burnished, it will never fade – most medieval manuscripts still shine brightly today.

Curling leaves are a popular "Gothic" design

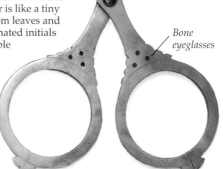

Bone eyeglasses

SIGHT FOR SORE EYES
Hours of close copying often damaged the eyesight. Europeans first started wearing eyeglasses in the 13th century. The invention of printing in the 1450s made more books available, and the sale of glasses rocketed.

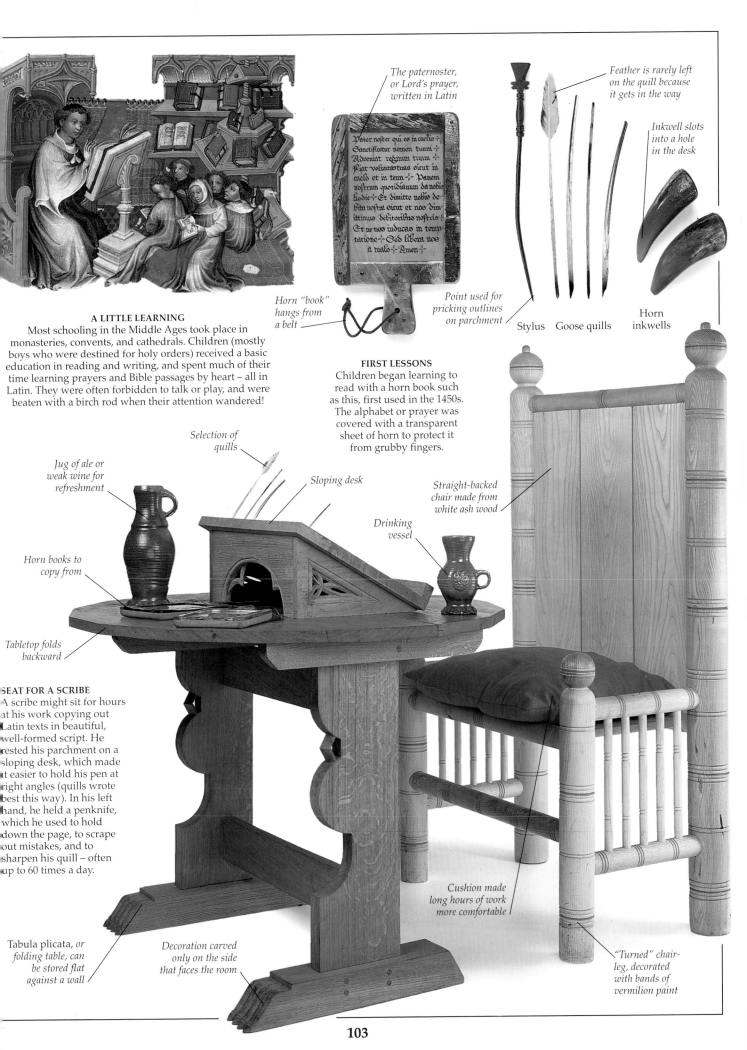

A LITTLE LEARNING

Most schooling in the Middle Ages took place in monasteries, convents, and cathedrals. Children (mostly boys who were destined for holy orders) received a basic education in reading and writing, and spent much of their time learning prayers and Bible passages by heart – all in Latin. They were often forbidden to talk or play, and were beaten with a birch rod when their attention wandered!

The paternoster, or Lord's prayer, written in Latin

Pater noster qui es in caelis✝
Sanctificetur nomen tuum ✝
Adveniat regnum tuum ✝
Fiat voluntas tua sicut in
caelo et in terra ✝ Panem
nostrum quotidianum da nobis
hodie ✝ Et dimitte nobis de
bita nostra sicut et nos dim
ittimus debitoribus nostris✝
Et ne nos inducas in temp
tatione ✝ Sed libera nos
a malo ✝ Amen ✝

Horn "book" hangs from a belt

Point used for pricking outlines on parchment

Feather is rarely left on the quill because it gets in the way

Inkwell slots into a hole in the desk

Stylus   Goose quills   Horn inkwells

FIRST LESSONS

Children began learning to read with a horn book such as this, first used in the 1450s. The alphabet or prayer was covered with a transparent sheet of horn to protect it from grubby fingers.

Selection of quills

Jug of ale or weak wine for refreshment

Sloping desk

Straight-backed chair made from white ash wood

Drinking vessel

Horn books to copy from

Tabletop folds backward

SEAT FOR A SCRIBE

A scribe might sit for hours at his work copying out Latin texts in beautiful, well-formed script. He rested his parchment on a sloping desk, which made it easier to hold his pen at right angles (quills wrote best this way). In his left hand, he held a penknife, which he used to hold down the page, to scrape out mistakes, and to sharpen his quill – often up to 60 times a day.

Tabula plicata, or folding table, can be stored flat against a wall

Decoration carved only on the side that faces the room

Cushion made long hours of work more comfortable

"Turned" chair-leg, decorated with bands of vermilion paint

Building a cathedral

IN THE EARLY MIDDLE AGES, large churches were built in the Roman style. They had massive pillars and thick walls to hold up the round-arched roofs. As a result, there were few windows, and Romanesque churches were sometimes dark and gloomy. By the 12th century, they were too small for the booming population of Europe, and for the growing stream of pilgrims (pp. 108–109). There was an explosion of cathedral building, starting in 1140 with the Abbey of St. Denis, near Paris. This was constructed in a startling new style, called Gothic, where the weight of the roof rested not on the walls, but on outside supports called buttresses. This allowed walls to be thinner, and pierced with tall windows that led the eye heavenward and flooded the cathedral with light.

SYMPHONIES IN STONE
Before 1350, 80 cathedrals were built in France alone. Among the first to use flying buttresses was Reims Cathedral, begun in 1211.

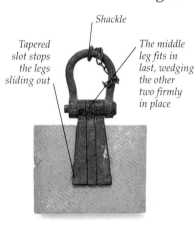

Shackle

Tapered slot stops the legs sliding out

The middle leg fits in last, wedging the other two firmly in place

LIFTING WITH A LEWIS
Medieval stonemasons (pp. 26–27) used lifting devices called lewises to raise heavy stone blocks. The legs fit into a tapered slot cut into the top of the stone (shown in cross section above), and the lifting rope is hooked onto the shackle at the top. This small modern lewis can lift blocks weighing up to a ton.

Windlass

Heavy stone blocks raised in a basket

Mortar carrier

Mason preparing blocks

MEN AT WORK
As the walls rose, masons had to work at greater heights. They stood on precarious wooden scaffolding lashed together with ropes. The stone was lifted up to them by a windlass, or hoist, attached to a big wheel turned by a man walking inside it. Working conditions were hazardous and there were many deaths.

Legs push outward as block is raised, so lewis does not fall out

Legs fit into a round hole

TIMELESS TOOLS
Lewises, like most other masonry tools (pp. 26–27), have changed little since medieval times. This kind of two-legged lewis was commonly used in the Middle Ages.

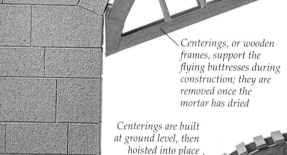

Centerings, or wooden frames, support the flying buttresses during construction; they are removed once the mortar has dried

Centerings are built at ground level, then hoisted into place

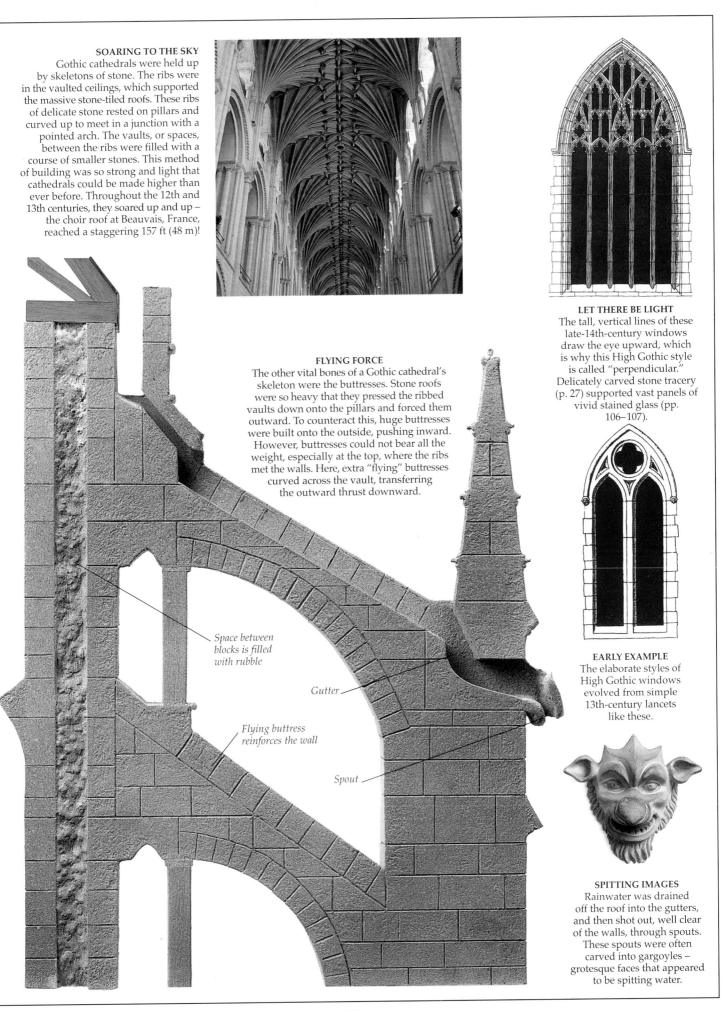

SOARING TO THE SKY
Gothic cathedrals were held up by skeletons of stone. The ribs were in the vaulted ceilings, which supported the massive stone-tiled roofs. These ribs of delicate stone rested on pillars and curved up to meet in a junction with a pointed arch. The vaults, or spaces, between the ribs were filled with a course of smaller stones. This method of building was so strong and light that cathedrals could be made higher than ever before. Throughout the 12th and 13th centuries, they soared up and up – the choir roof at Beauvais, France, reached a staggering 157 ft (48 m)!

FLYING FORCE
The other vital bones of a Gothic cathedral's skeleton were the buttresses. Stone roofs were so heavy that they pressed the ribbed vaults down onto the pillars and forced them outward. To counteract this, huge buttresses were built onto the outside, pushing inward. However, buttresses could not bear all the weight, especially at the top, where the ribs met the walls. Here, extra "flying" buttresses curved across the vault, transferring the outward thrust downward.

Space between blocks is filled with rubble

Gutter

Flying buttress reinforces the wall

Spout

LET THERE BE LIGHT
The tall, vertical lines of these late-14th-century windows draw the eye upward, which is why this High Gothic style is called "perpendicular." Delicately carved stone tracery (p. 27) supported vast panels of vivid stained glass (pp. 106–107).

EARLY EXAMPLE
The elaborate styles of High Gothic windows evolved from simple 13th-century lancets like these.

SPITTING IMAGES
Rainwater was drained off the roof into the gutters, and then shot out, well clear of the walls, through spouts. These spouts were often carved into gargoyles – grotesque faces that appeared to be spitting water.

The art of decoration

"I AM A POOR OLD WOMAN who knows nothing, who cannot read. But in the Church I see Paradise painted, and Hell where the damned broil." These were the words of a 15th-century French woman, and they spoke for millions of uneducated people in medieval Europe. For them, cathedrals and churches were not just places of worship, they were picture books and art galleries. The great cathedrals were filled with statues and carvings, painted panels and frescoes, which told stories of saints and biblical characters. Most wonderful of all were the stained glass windows through which light streamed in dazzling, brilliant colors.

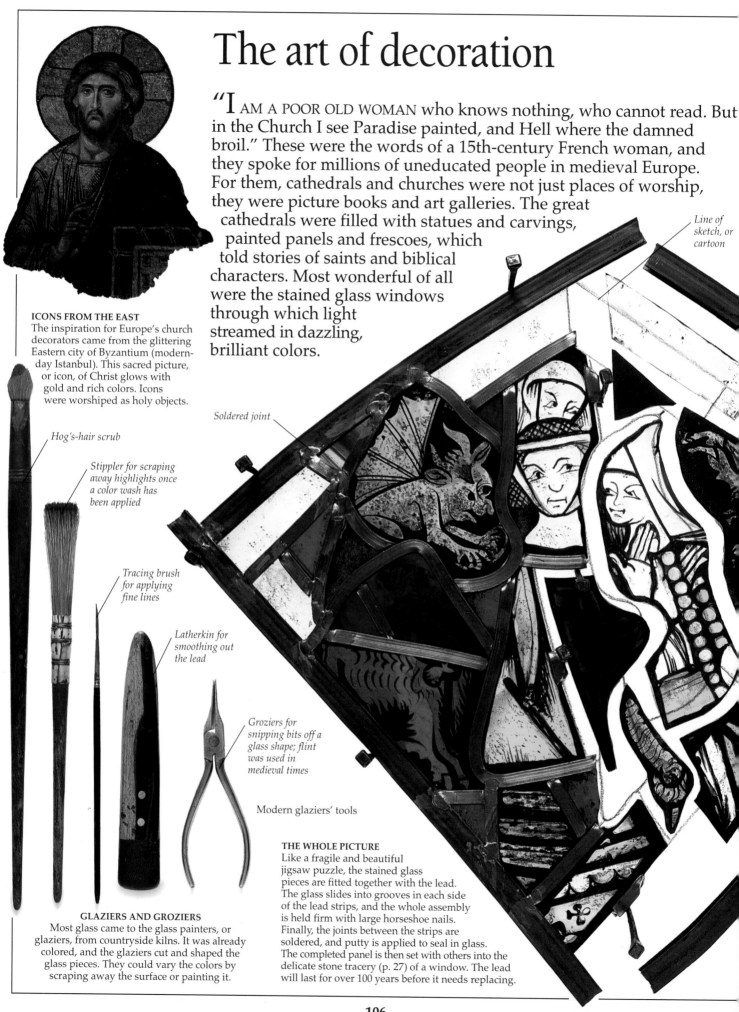

ICONS FROM THE EAST
The inspiration for Europe's church decorators came from the glittering Eastern city of Byzantium (modern-day Istanbul). This sacred picture, or icon, of Christ glows with gold and rich colors. Icons were worshiped as holy objects.

Hog's-hair scrub

Stippler for scraping away highlights once a color wash has been applied

Tracing brush for applying fine lines

Latherkin for smoothing out the lead

Groziers for snipping bits off a glass shape; flint was used in medieval times

Modern glaziers' tools

Line of sketch, or cartoon

Soldered joint

GLAZIERS AND GROZIERS
Most glass came to the glass painters, or glaziers, from countryside kilns. It was already colored, and the glaziers cut and shaped the glass pieces. They could vary the colors by scraping away the surface or painting it.

THE WHOLE PICTURE
Like a fragile and beautiful jigsaw puzzle, the stained glass pieces are fitted together with the lead. The glass slides into grooves in each side of the lead strips, and the whole assembly is held firm with large horseshoe nails. Finally, the joints between the strips are soldered, and putty is applied to seal in glass. The completed panel is then set with others into the delicate stone tracery (p. 27) of a window. The lead will last for over 100 years before it needs replacing.

Wicked devil urges on the three gossips

Line of clear glass was known as the white, or sacrificial, line, because it was most likely to be broken when the panel was removed for re-leading

Cut and painted glass shape

STORIES IN GLASS
Stained glass windows were like cartoon strips. Through pictures, they taught religious lessons and the stories of the Bible to those who could not read. This panel depicts three gossiping women with leering devils at their shoulders. The moral is clear – don't speak badly of your neighbors!

CUT AND COLORED
In medieval times, the design for a window was drawn onto a board coated with chalk and water. Glass pieces were placed over the design and cut to shape, using a hot iron to score the glass. Final trimming was done by nibbling the edges with a grozier. The details of the picture were painted on with enamel, and the glass was fired to fuse in the paint.

Space left for lead is called the "cut line"

The lead has grooves along each side into which the glass fits

Large nails hold the jigsaw of glass and lead together before soldering

Lead is soft and can be shaped around the glass quite easily

Charlemagne (p. 6) was a renowned Christian king

BEAUTIFUL BLUE
Medieval glassmakers produced colors by adding metallic oxides to the molten glass. The glowing colors they created were named after precious stones – ruby red, emerald green, and sapphire blue. The recipes for different colors were closely guarded secrets and most have since been lost. The beautiful blue glass in these famous windows at Chartres Cathedral, France, was known as *bleu de ciel* – "heavenly blue."

A SHINING EXAMPLE
Altarpieces usually portrayed great moments from the story of Christ. This altar panel was painted in 1333 for Siena Cathedral, Italy, by Simone Martini and Lippo Memmi. It shows the Archangel Gabriel announcing to Mary that she will bear the baby Jesus. The style is much more natural than the stiff and formal design of Byzantine icons. The central figures, glowing against a golden background, are full of graceful movement.

An altarpiece is set behind the altar

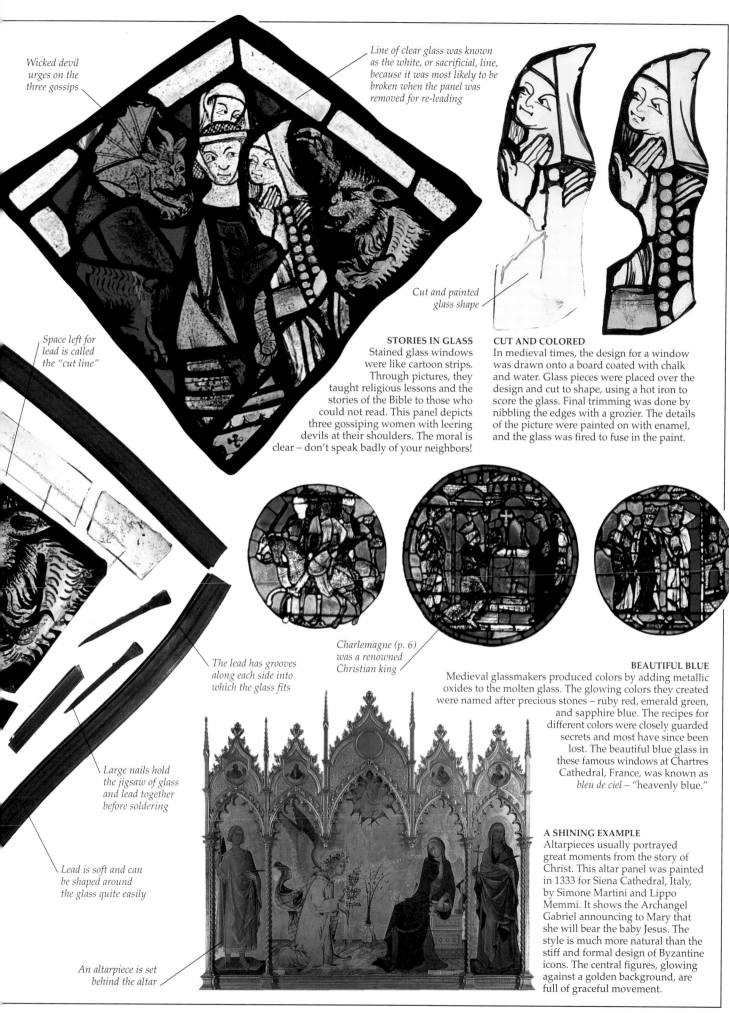

Saints and pilgrims

Most people in the Middle Ages hoped to go on a pilgrimage to a holy shrine at some point in their lives. They went for many reasons – as proof of their devotion to God, as an act of penance for their sins, or to find a cure for an illness. The holy city of Jerusalem was a favorite destination, as were Rome, where both St. Peter and St. Paul were believed to be buried, the shrine of St. James at Santiago de Compostela in Spain, and Canterbury Cathedral in England. On the road, rich and poor traveled together, and for many, pilgrimages were a sort of holiday. To pass the time, people sang songs and hymns, played pipes, and told stories over their evening meals in roadside taverns.

ON THE ROAD
In the early Middle Ages, most pilgrims traveled on foot. They wore long woolen tunics called sclaveins, broad-brimmed felt hats, and sandals.

Front part of reliquary contains a holy cross set in pearls and rock crystal

Scallop-shell emblem of Santiago de Compostela

Tiny flask, or ampulla, for holy water

Pewter badge of St. Thomas Becket

PORTABLE RELICS
Holy relics, or the bones of saints, were not only kept in shrines. People carried them in bags around their necks or in beautifully decorated cases like this one. Knights often had relics placed in their sword hilts.

SIGN OF THE SHRINE
Like modern tourists, medieval pilgrims often sported badges to show that they had been to a certain shrine. They wore them on their hats to make it clear that they were on a holy journey and had the right to protection. The scallop shell was a popular emblem.

Back part of reliquary contains pieces of bone, or relics, set in gold as a sign of their value

Figure of Christ

Becket's body is laid in a shroud

Becket is carried to Heaven by angels

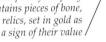

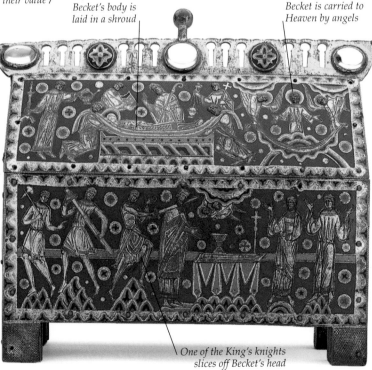

A MARTYR'S BONES
This 12th-century reliquary casket depicts the murder of Archbishop Thomas Becket (on Henry II's orders) in Canterbury Cathedral in 1170. Becket became a saint, and Canterbury, resting place of his bones, quickly became a place of pilgrimage.

One of the King's knights slices off Becket's head

THE PILGRIM'S POET
Geoffrey Chaucer (c. 1340–1400) wrote the best-loved book about pilgrims, *The Canterbury Tales*. It is a series of stories in verse told by a party of 30 pilgrims to pass the time as they ride to Canterbury. The pilgrims, who include a knight, a miller, a friar, a prioress, and a cook, portray a vivid and often hilarious picture of medieval life.

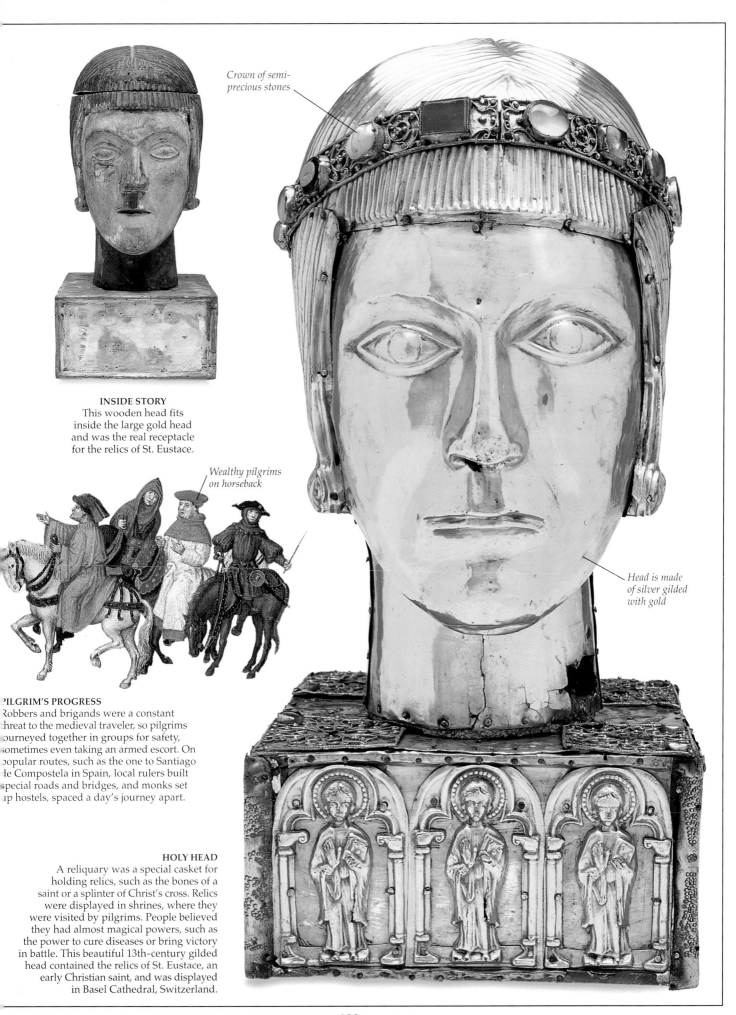

INSIDE STORY
This wooden head fits inside the large gold head and was the real receptacle for the relics of St. Eustace.

Crown of semi-precious stones

Wealthy pilgrims on horseback

Head is made of silver gilded with gold

PILGRIM'S PROGRESS
Robbers and brigands were a constant threat to the medieval traveler, so pilgrims journeyed together in groups for safety, sometimes even taking an armed escort. On popular routes, such as the one to Santiago de Compostela in Spain, local rulers built special roads and bridges, and monks set up hostels, spaced a day's journey apart.

HOLY HEAD
A reliquary was a special casket for holding relics, such as the bones of a saint or a splinter of Christ's cross. Relics were displayed in shrines, where they were visited by pilgrims. People believed they had almost magical powers, such as the power to cure diseases or bring victory in battle. This beautiful 13th-century gilded head contained the relics of St. Eustace, an early Christian saint, and was displayed in Basel Cathedral, Switzerland.

The Islamic world

THE PROPHET MUHAMMAD, founder of Islam, died in 632. Within 100 years, Arab armies had conquered a vast empire that stretched from Spain and North Africa to Persia and India. International trade flourished in the Islamic world, spreading ideas as well as goods. Muslim scientists became particularly advanced in the fields of medicine and mathematics: they were skilled surgeons and eye doctors, invented algebra (from the Arabic *al-jebr*), and introduced the Arabic numeral system to Europe, a version of which is still in use today. Although the Christians saw the Muslims as an "infidel" race and an almost inhuman enemy during the Crusades, they learned much from this highly advanced civilization as trade links grew stronger.

GLITTERING PRIZE
The rich cities of the Islamic world were prime targets for the plundering crusaders (p. 42). In 1099, they succeeded in overrunning the holy city of Jerusalem, killing its inhabitants, and pillaging its vast treasures.

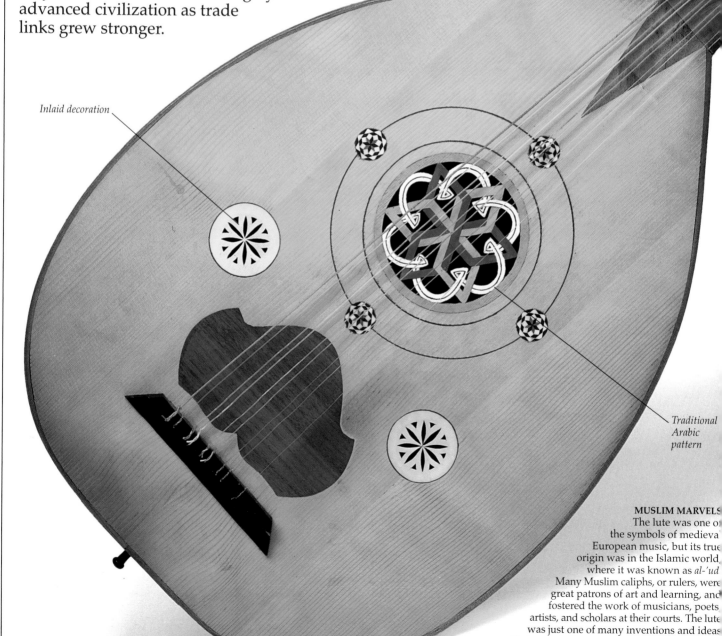

Inlaid decoration

Traditional Arabic pattern

MUSLIM MARVELS
The lute was one of the symbols of medieval European music, but its true origin was in the Islamic world, where it was known as *al-'ud*. Many Muslim caliphs, or rulers, were great patrons of art and learning, and fostered the work of musicians, poets, artists, and scholars at their courts. The lute was just one of many inventions and ideas that came to Europe from the Muslim empire.

LUXURY TRAIN

Camel trains carried a huge range of goods across the deserts and mountains of the Islamic world. In the dazzling bazaars of Baghdad and Damascus, the wealthy could buy a stunning variety of luxury goods, from Persian carpets and African ivory, to Asian silks, spices, jewels, and furs.

HEAVENLY GUIDANCE

The Muslims were brilliant astronomers. They developed the astrolabe, which enabled travelers to fix their position by studying the night sky. Camel drivers used this instrument to navigate across the desert, and Europeans soon copied the idea and used it for finding their way at sea.

HERO OF A HOLY WAR

Saladin (1137–1193) was a great Islamic sultan who led the Muslim armies against the crusaders, and recaptured Jerusalem. He was respected even by his enemies as a brilliant general and a wise man.

MEDICINE MEN

Even as the Crusades were raging, Europeans learned a great deal from Islamic doctors, whose knowledge was far in advance of their own. Cures for numerous ills could be bought in apothecaries such as this. In the 11th century, the great Arab doctor Avicenna (980–1037) wrote a medical encyclopedia that became the single greatest influence on medieval medicine.

ARTS AND CRAFTS

Islamic craftsmen were renowned for their beautiful enamel work. They usually decorated religious artifacts, such as this 13th-century mosque lamp, with Arabic words and geometric patterns, because Islamic tradition banned images of human figures and other living things from religious buildings.

The Crusades

IN 1095 AT CLERMONT, FRANCE, Pope Urban II launched a military expedition to take the Christian holy places in Jerusalem back from the Seljuk Turks who ruled the Holy Land. This expedition became known as the First Crusade. A huge army traveled thousands of miles across Europe, gathering at Constantinople (now Istanbul) before going on to capture Jerusalem in 1099. But the city was soon retaken by the Muslims, and many other crusades failed to take it back, apart from a brief period in 1228-29 when the German emperor Frederick II made an agreement with the Muslims. Even Richard Lionheart, the warlike English king and a leader of the Third Crusade of 1189–1192, knew that if he could capture the city, he would not be able to hold it. Nevertheless, Western leaders set up feudal states in the Holy Land. The fall of Acre in 1291 marked the end of one of these states. But Christians still fought Muslims in Spain and the Mediterranean. Crusades were also preached against non-Catholic heretics in Europe.

PEOPLE'S CRUSADE
In 1096 the French preacher Peter the Hermit led an undisciplined mob from Cologne in Germany toward Jerusalem. On their way they pillaged and looted, killing Jews for their money and because they thought them responsible for Christ's death. Though there were some knights in this People's Crusade, it was wiped out in Anatolia (modern Turkey) by the Turks.

SPANISH CRUSADERS
Muslims, known as Moors, had lived in Spain since the eighth century. From the 11th century on, Christian armies tried to push them back south; Granada, their last stronghold, fell to the Christians in 1492. Warrior monks, such as the Order of Santiago, seen in this 13th-century picture, helped the Christian reconquest of Spain.

TAKING SHIP
To get from Europe to the Holy Land, people could either take the dangerous road overland, or cross the Mediterranean Sea. The Italian city-states of Venice, Pisa, and Genoa, eager for new trade, often provided ships. Unfortunately, in 1203 Venice persuaded the leaders of the Fourth Crusade to attack the Byzantine capital of Constantinople, which never recovered.

THE MAMLUKS
An elite body of troops, the Mamluks were slaves recruited by the Muslims. This late 13th- or early 14th-century bronze bowl shows a mounted Mamluk heavy cavalryman. He appears to be wearing a lamellar cuirass, a type of armor that was made from small iron plates laced together. Above his head he holds a slightly curved saber.

Border of crowns

KING ON A TITLE
Medieval churches were often decorated with patterned ceramic tiles. These examples come from Chertsey Abbey, England. They bear a portrait of Richard I, known as Richard Lionheart, who was king of England from 1189 to 1199, and was one of the leaders of the Third Crusade of 1190.

Mamluk cavalryman

Arabic inscription

A SARACEN
Many Saracens (nomadic Muslims) used fast horses and shot arrows at the Crusaders from their recurved composite bows. Some wore forms of plate armor but many wore mail or padded defenses. Round shields were common, and curved slashing sabers became popular in the 12th century.

TURKISH WARRIOR
This Italian dish of about 1520 shows a Turkish warrior. The crusades died out in the early 14th century and the great fortified city of Constantinople (now Istanbul) stood between Turkey and the mainland of Europe. However, the city never fully recovered from the damage it suffered during the Fourth Crusade in 1204. In 1453 it finally fell to the Sultan Suleyman the Magnificent. It has remained part of Turkey ever since.

FIGHTING FOR THE FAITH
This mid-13th-century picture shows Christians and Muslims clashing in 1218 during the Christian siege of Damietta at the mouth of the Nile in Egypt. The artist has dressed the Muslims (on the right) much like Christians.

STRONGHOLDS IN THE EAST
The Crusaders built stone castles and borrowed some ideas from examples in the East. Crusader castles were built on strong natural sites when possible. This huge castle, Krak des Chevaliers in Syria, was held by the Knights Hospitalers. An outer ring of walls was added in the 13th century.

CROSS-LEGGED KNIGHT
This effigy, carved in the late 13th century, was said to be that of English knight Sir John Holcombe, who died of wounds during the Second Crusade (1147-1149). The cross-legged pose is often thought to indicate a Crusader. In fact it is simply a style used by the sculptors of the time.

Crusader castles

For over 200 years European Christians fought the Muslims to try to win control of the Holy Land by launching expeditions called Crusades. They were impressed by huge Byzantine and Muslim fortifications and took over Muslim strongholds to encourage European settlers. They built castles to guard roads and to help them attack nearby towns. By the late 12th century such castles were being used as border posts, administrative centers, safe havens, and army bases. Often, the Crusaders used ideal sites for castles, places protected on three sides by a sea or river; they built strong walls and ditches to guard the fourth side. When, rapid building was necessary, so simple rectangular enclosures with corner and flanking towers were raised.

BESIEGED
This 13th-century Italian manuscript shows Crusaders trying to break into Antioch. This city was so large that the men of the First Crusade (1095–1099) could not surround it, in spite of the size of their army. So they had to guard against sorties (p. 85) from the gates, building forts to watch over them. European artists knew that the crescent was a Muslim symbol, and thought it was used on the defenders' shields.

Battlements

Main tower

Small window

MAILED KNIGHT
Crusaders, like this knight of about 1280, wore a shirt of mail, a cloth surcoat, and a helm on the head.

POOR KNIGHTS?
The seal of the Knights Templar shows two knights on one horse, suggesting their original poverty. This order of warrior-monks was formed in 1119. They took their name from their headquarters, which was near the Temple in Jerusalem.

KERAK
This castle stands on a narrow neck of land in the Jordanian desert. It is isolated from the nearby town, and from the approach at the other end, by ditches cut in the rock. The other sides have natural steep rock slopes. A lower courtyard on one side gave the defenders two levels from which to fire. Built in 1142, it was so effective in disrupting the communications of the Muslims that it was attacked several times. It took an eight-month siege by the Muslim leader Saladin in 118[ ] before the castle fe[ ]

Wall of lower courtyard

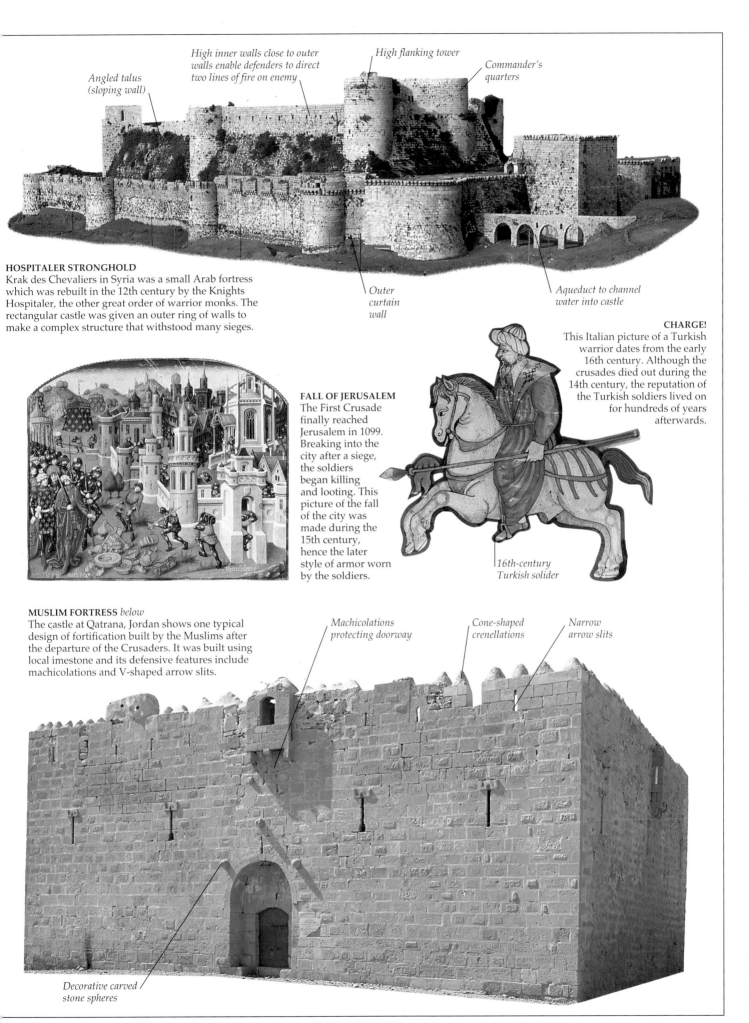

High inner walls close to outer
walls enable defenders to direct
two lines of fire on enemy

Angled talus
(sloping wall)

High flanking tower

Commander's
quarters

Outer
curtain
wall

Aqueduct to channel
water into castle

HOSPITALER STRONGHOLD
Krak des Chevaliers in Syria was a small Arab fortress
which was rebuilt in the 12th century by the Knights
Hospitaler, the other great order of warrior monks. The
rectangular castle was given an outer ring of walls to
make a complex structure that withstood many sieges.

FALL OF JERUSALEM
The First Crusade
finally reached
Jerusalem in 1099.
Breaking into the
city after a siege,
the soldiers
began killing
and looting. This
picture of the fall
of the city was
made during the
15th century,
hence the later
style of armor worn
by the soldiers.

CHARGE!
This Italian picture of a Turkish
warrior dates from the early
16th century. Although the
crusades died out during the
14th century, the reputation of
the Turkish soldiers lived on
for hundreds of years
afterwards.

16th-century
Turkish solider

MUSLIM FORTRESS *below*
The castle at Qatrana, Jordan shows one typical
design of fortification built by the Muslims after
the departure of the Crusaders. It was built using
local imestone and its defensive features include
machicolations and V-shaped arrow slits.

Machicolations
protecting doorway

Cone-shaped
crenellations

Narrow
arrow slits

Decorative carved
stone spheres

Knights of Christ

IN 1118 A BAND OF KNIGHTS who protected Christian pilgrims in the Holy Land were given quarters near the Temple of Jerusalem. These men, the Knights Templars ("of the temple"), became a religious order but differed from other monks by remaining warriors and continuing to fight the Muslims. In the same period another order of monks, who had worked with the sick, became a military order called the Knights of St. John or Knights Hospitalers. When the Christians lost control of the Holy Land in 1291 the Templars, by now less active, found that the European rulers who had supported them did not like their wealth, power, and their lack of action, and they were disbanded. The Hospitalers moved their base to the Mediterranean and continued fighting the Muslims. The Teutonic Knights, a German order that had become military in 1198, moved to Eastern Europe and forced the Slavs to convert to Christianity.

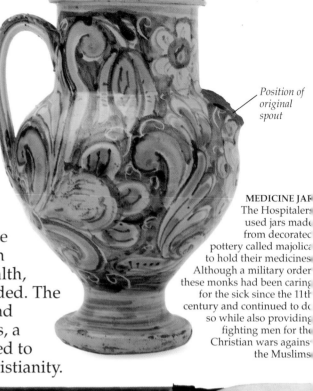

Position of original spout

MEDICINE JAR
The Hospitalers used jars made from decorated pottery called majolica to hold their medicines. Although a military order, these monks had been caring for the sick since the 11th century and continued to do so while also providing fighting men for the Christian wars against the Muslims.

THE HOSPITAL
Malta was the final home of the Knights of St. John. This engraving of 1586 shows them at work on the great ward of their hospital in the Maltese capital, Valletta.

BRONZE MORTAR
Ingredients for Hospitaler medicines were ground by a pestle in this mortar dating from the 12th or 13th century.

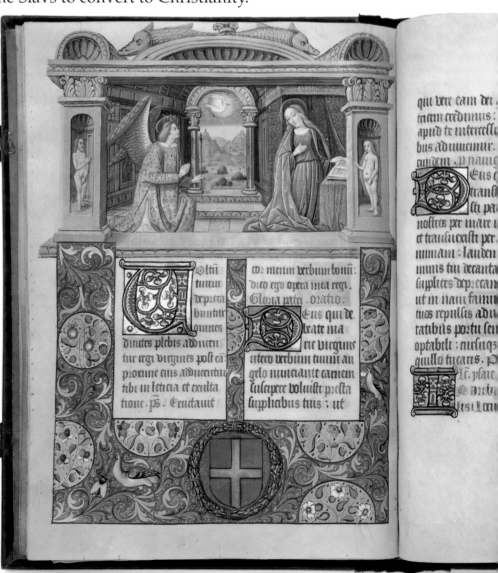

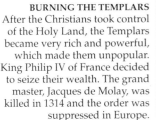
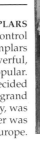

BURNING THE TEMPLARS

After the Christians took control of the Holy Land, the Templars became very rich and powerful, which made them unpopular. King Philip IV of France decided to seize their wealth. The grand master, Jacques de Molay, was killed in 1314 and the order was suppressed in Europe.

THE FIGHT GOES ON

After the loss of the Holy Land in 1291, the Hospitalers moved first to Cyprus, then in 1310 to Rhodes where they again clashed with the Muslims. This continual struggle meant that despite their wealth, they managed to escape the fate of the Templars.

GRAND MASTER'S SEAL

A grand master led each military order. This seal belonged to Raymond de Berenger, who ruled the Hospitalers from 1363–1374.

PROCESSIONAL CROSS

This early 16th-century cross is made of oak covered with silver plate. The figure of Christ is older. The Evangelists are pictured on the arms of the cross. The cross belonged to the Hospitalers and the coat of arms is that of Pierre Decluys, Grand Prior of France from 1522–1535. Each military order had priories or commanderies in several countries to raise money and recruits.

ORDER OF SERVICE *above*

The Knights of St. John were expected to attend church services and to know their Bible in the same way as other monks. Breviaries like this one contained the daily service. The religious knights had to obey strict rules, which were usually based on those of the regular monastic orders. Hospitalers followed the rule of St. Benedict, the Templars that of the Cistercian order.

KNIGHT TEMPLAR

Templars wore a white surcoat (tunic) with a red cross. In this 12th-century fresco from the Templar church at Cressac, France, a knight gallops into battle.

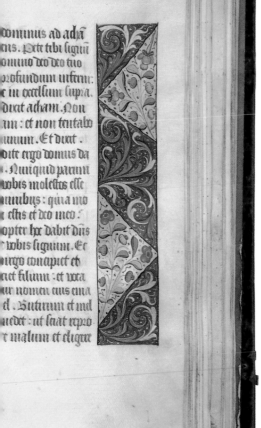

THE RHODES MISSAL

Joining the Knights Hospitaler meant being a skilled fighting man yet rejecting the world for a monastic life. Like other monks, the knights swore to serve the order faithfully, to remain chaste, and to help those in need. It is thought that many knights took their vows on this book, the late-15th-century Rhodes Missal.

WATER BOTTLE

A water supply was vital in the heat of the Mediterranean and along pilgrim routes in the Holy Land. This metal water bottle of about 1500 bears the cross of the Order of St. John.

Knights of the Rising Sun

EUROPE WAS NOT the only area to have a warrior class. Japan developed a society similar to the feudal system of medieval Europe, and the equivalent of the knight was the samurai. Like a Western knight he was a warrior, often fighting on horseback, serving a lord and served by others in turn. After the Gempei War of 1180-1185 Japan was ruled by an emperor, but real power lay with the shogun, or military leader. However, civil wars had weakened the Shogun's power by 1550, and Japan was split into kingdoms ruled by daimyo or barons. In 1543 Portuguese merchants brought the first guns to Japan; soon large, professional armies appeared. A strong shogun was revived after a victory in 1600, and the last great samurai battle was fought in 1615.

HELMET AND FACE GUARD
Helmets like this 17th-century example are often fitted with mustaches. They have a neckguard made of iron plates coated with lacquer (a type of varnish) and laced together with silk. Lacquer was used to protect metal from moisture in the humid climate of Japan.

SWORDSMAN
Samurai prized their swords greatly. This 19th-century print shows a samurai holding his long sword unsheathed. His smaller sword is thrust through his belt, with the cutting edge uppermost to deliver a blow straight from the scabbard.

FIGHTING SAMURAI
These two samurai are fighting on foot. From the 14th century on, there was an increase in this type of combat, although samurai still fought on horseback when necessary. The shift toward foot combat with sword and curved spear brought changes in the armor.

EARLY ARMOR *above*
This 19th-century copy of a 12th-century armor is in the *O-yoroi*, or "great armor," style. An iron strip is attached to the top of the breast, and the rest of the cuirass is made of small lacquered iron plates laced together with silk and leather. The 12th-century samurai who wore armor like this were basically mounted archers.

Tempered edge

PAIR OF SWORDS
The main samurai sword was the *katana*, sheathed in a wooden scabbard (*saya*). The guard for the hilt was formed by a decorated oval metal plate (*tsuba*). The grip (*tsuka*) was covered in rough sharkskin, to prevent the hand slipping, and bound with silk braid. A pommel cap (*kashira*) fitted over the end. The pair of swords (*daisho*) was completed by a shorter sword (*wakizashi*), which was also stuck through the belt.

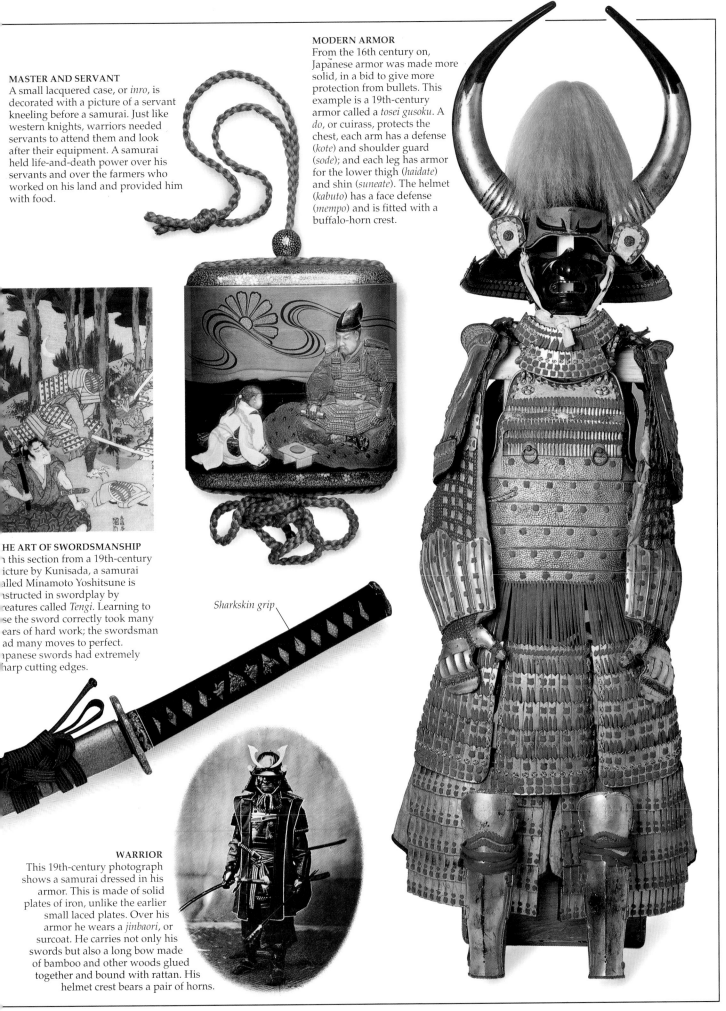

MASTER AND SERVANT

A small lacquered case, or *inro*, is decorated with a picture of a servant kneeling before a samurai. Just like western knights, warriors needed servants to attend them and look after their equipment. A samurai held life-and-death power over his servants and over the farmers who worked on his land and provided him with food.

MODERN ARMOR

From the 16th century on, Japanese armor was made more solid, in a bid to give more protection from bullets. This example is a 19th-century armor called a *tosei gusoku*. A *do*, or cuirass, protects the chest, each arm has a defense (*kote*) and shoulder guard (*sode*); and each leg has armor for the lower thigh (*haidate*) and shin (*suneate*). The helmet (*kabuto*) has a face defense (*mempo*) and is fitted with a buffalo-horn crest.

THE ART OF SWORDSMANSHIP

In this section from a 19th-century picture by Kunisada, a samurai called Minamoto Yoshitsune is instructed in swordplay by creatures called *Tengi*. Learning to use the sword correctly took many years of hard work; the swordsman had many moves to perfect. Japanese swords had extremely sharp cutting edges.

Sharkskin grip

WARRIOR

This 19th-century photograph shows a samurai dressed in his armor. This is made of solid plates of iron, unlike the earlier small laced plates. Over his armor he wears a *jinbaori*, or surcoat. He carries not only his swords but also a long bow made of bamboo and other woods glued together and bound with rattan. His helmet crest bears a pair of horns.

Castles in Japan

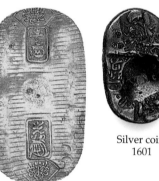

FORTRESSES HAD BEEN BUILT in Japan since the Yamato period (A.D. 300–710). Sometimes these were temporary strongholds, but by the 14th century more permanent fortifications of wood were beginning to appear. The 16th and early 17th centuries, a time when castles were in decline in Europe, saw the heyday of castles in Japan. The reasons for this were the political instability in Japan and the use of small firearms. Cannons were not highly developed there, so warriors could shelter behind castle walls, safe against the handguns and cavalry of their enemies. Natural hill sites were used if possible; otherwise platforms of rammed earth were built and faced with smooth stone blocks. Rivers, lakes, or the sea provided natural moats.

MANY BAILEYS
Castles often contained many courtyards, which kept the main tower a safe distance from attempts to set it on fire. Progress through the courtyards was sometimes like going through a maze. An attacker would have to go through all the baileys before getting to the main tower.

NEW MONEY
Ieyasu was first of the Tokugawa shoguns, imperial officials who became the most powerful men in Japan. He reorganized Japan's monetary system in the late 16th century, using cast or beaten slabs of gold or silver for coins.

Silver coin, 1601

Gold coin, 1601

SWORD POLISHING
Polishers work on lethally sharp samurai weapons. In the later 16th century, samurai warriors often lived in large castles, as the daimyos (provincial rulers) began to replace their many small fortresses with single huge castles, often built in towns. Such castles became administrative centers as well as fortresses.

SAMURAI
The samurai was in many ways similar to the feudal knight of Europe. He was a trained warrior who served a lord and expected to be served by peasants and merchants. His armor was made in a unique way. It consisted of iron plates laced together. Because of the damp climate the iron was lacquered to keep it from rusting. This armor was effective against the very sharp swords that were the mark of the samurai. This picture shows a samurai warrior crossing the Uji River in 1184.

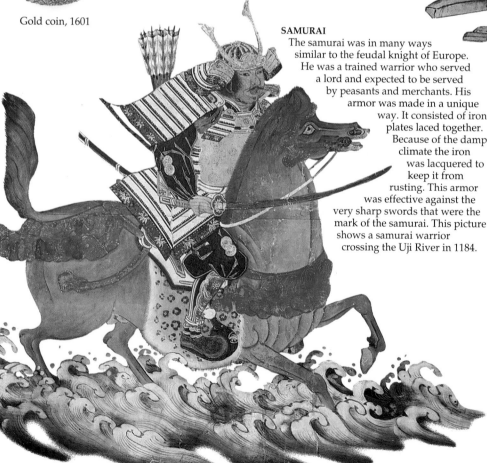

ATTACKING THE GATE
The assault on the Sanjo palace (1160) shows a common method of attack. This was rarely successful, unlike starvation or betrayal. Sometimes the garrison shot the attackers in the courtyard. Siege techniques were similar to those used in Europe, although mines were not used until the later 16th century.

There were often several towers in a castle to allow the defenders to fire on the enemy from different angles. The gates also often had single-story towers over them. The heart of the castle was the main tower which, built on an earthen mound, was several stories high. In later castles the base was protected by stone, and the structure above was made of wood. To reduce the fire risk, wooden parts of the towers were often thickly plastered and the gates covered with iron plates. Towers like this one at Himeji castle served as command centers, watchtowers, and storage areas. In the upper floors were quarters for the lord.

Highly decorated gable indicates the great power of the lord

Wooden upper story

BADGE
Family badges were known as "mon." They were painted on items such as armor and banners. This is the butterfly mon of the Ashikaga family.

Pagoda-like roof with broad overhang

Narrow window openings

Roof of wooden shingles

Plastered outer wall

Inner wooden framework

Gun loop

Ground floor protected by dressed stone slabs

121

Castles in decline

BY THE END OF THE 15TH CENTURY, castles were losing their military importance. Societies gradually became more stable, and people demanded more comfortable living conditions. Gunpowder appeared in Europe in the early 14th century but did not have any great effect on castles at first – they were still being built 200 years later. From the 16th century on, some castles continued in military use, especially in danger areas such as Austria, a buffer zone protecting western Europe from the Turks. Other castles were used as army barracks. Fortified tower-houses were still built in places such as Scotland and Ireland, where riots or raids by neighbors made protection necessary. But many castles fell into ruin; the stone was even stolen and used in buildings elsewhere. In the 18th and 19th centuries there was new interest in castles as symbols of the medieval world.

EXPLOSIVE PIONEER
Roger Bacon was a Franciscan monk who lived in England and France in the 13th century. He was particularly well known for his writings on science and technology and was the first Western writer to describe how to make gunpowder. His recipe appeared in a book published in 1242.

TURKS ATTACK
In 1453 the Turks managed to break into the heavily fortified city of Constantinople (now Istanbul), which was one of the last strongholds of the Christian Byzantine empire. The formidable walls were attacked by land and sea, and the Turks used numerous guns to make holes in the walls.

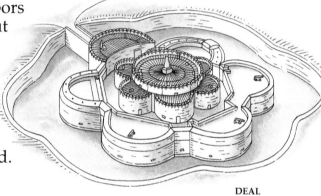

DEAL
The fort at Deal, England, was built by Henry VIII in the 1530s as part of a chain of similar defenses on the English coast. The low, rounded gun platforms deflect enemy missiles and present less of a target to cannons, but fortifications using arrowhead-shaped bastions were already taking over in Europe.

VASE GUN
The earliest pictures of cannons are English and appear in 1326. They show a vase-shaped object which would have been strapped down to a wooden stand. Such guns shot large metal darts and may have been aimed at doors to frighten defenders and keep them from coming out.

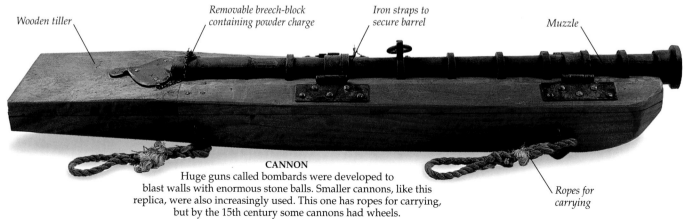

Wooden tiller

Removable breech-block containing powder charge

Iron straps to secure barrel

Muzzle

Ropes for carrying

CANNON
Huge guns called bombards were developed to blast walls with enormous stone balls. Smaller cannons, like this replica, were also increasingly used. This one has ropes for carrying, but by the 15th century some cannons had wheels.

FAIRY-TALE CASTLE
The German castle of Neuschwanstein was
built by King Ludwig of Bavaria in the late 19th
century. It is one of several 19th-century castles
created by people who were influenced by a
romantic image of the medieval world.

Notch in
which to
rest gun

Copy of late
14th-centry
handgun

Wooden
pavise, or
portable
shield

Heraldic
badge to
identify the
lord of this
marksman

Iron
barrel

Steel
kettle-hat

Coat of
plates, a
garment
lined with
steel plates
riveted
inside

Steel
buckler, or
fist-shield

Wooden
prop

Steel spike to stop
shield slipping

HANDGUNNER
Early handguns were fired either by a hot wire
pressed against the touch-hole, or by a glowing slow match
made from cord soaked in saltpeter (potassium nitrate). Some guns
had a lug on the bottom to hook over walls and absorb recoil. Inside a
castle, guns could be fired through round loopholes in the walls or
long horizontal slots for larger weapons, which would be fired at a
besieger's cannons or earthworks. Later, guns were often arranged in
groups, and this technique led to the building of forts that could hold
batteries of guns. Unlike medieval castles, these forts
were usually built and run by the state.

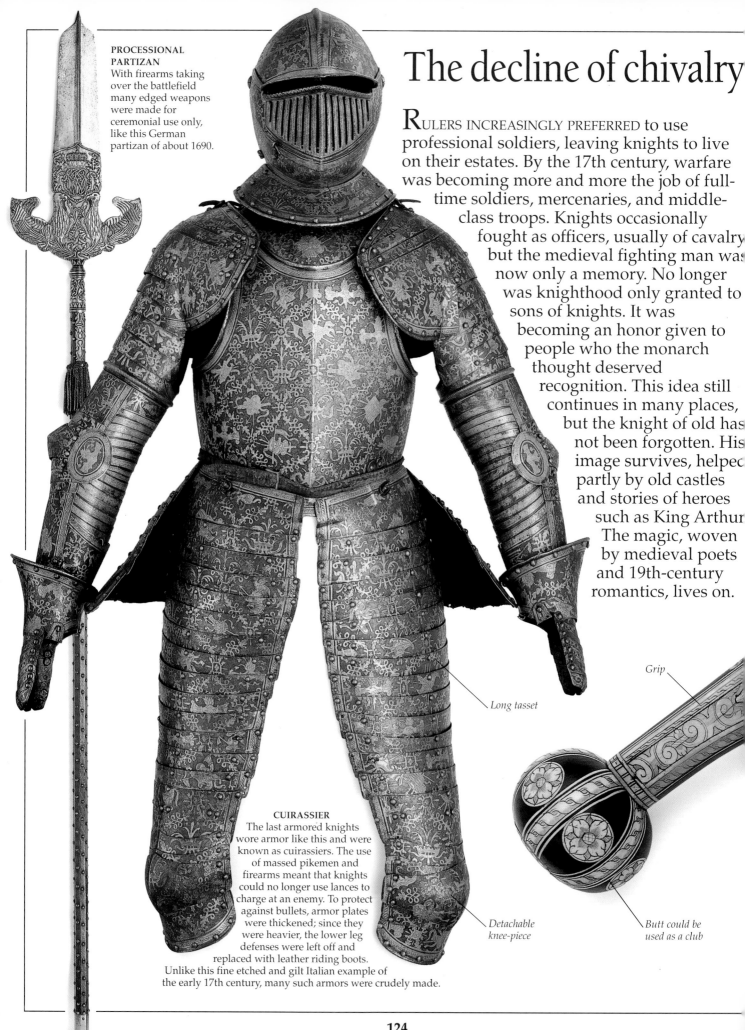

PROCESSIONAL PARTIZAN
With firearms taking over the battlefield many edged weapons were made for ceremonial use only, like this German partizan of about 1690.

RULERS INCREASINGLY PREFERRED to use professional soldiers, leaving knights to live on their estates. By the 17th century, warfare was becoming more and more the job of full-time soldiers, mercenaries, and middle-class troops. Knights occasionally fought as officers, usually of cavalry, but the medieval fighting man was now only a memory. No longer was knighthood only granted to sons of knights. It was becoming an honor given to people who the monarch thought deserved recognition. This idea still continues in many places, but the knight of old has not been forgotten. His image survives, helped partly by old castles and stories of heroes such as King Arthur. The magic, woven by medieval poets and 19th-century romantics, lives on.

Grip

Long tasset

CUIRASSIER
The last armored knights wore armor like this and were known as cuirassiers. The use of massed pikemen and firearms meant that knights could no longer use lances to charge at an enemy. To protect against bullets, armor plates were thickened; since they were heavier, the lower leg defenses were left off and replaced with leather riding boots. Unlike this fine etched and gilt Italian example of the early 17th century, many such armors were crudely made.

Detachable knee-piece

Butt could be used as a club

OLD VERSUS NEW *right*
This engraving of 1632 shows how an armored cuirassier with a lance could be stopped by an infantryman with a musket. Notice the wheel-lock pistol, a more effective weapon for the horseman, hanging in its holster from the saddle.

PREPARING TO FIRE *left*
An early-17th-century Dutch musketeer pours a measured amount of gunpowder from his powder flask into his musket.

BUFF COAT
Light cavalrymen found that a coat of soft, thick buff leather was able to stop a sword cut and was more comfortable than full armor. It was worn either alone or with a breastplate and backplate. At this time, breastplates were usually "proofed," or tested, by being shot at before they were worn.

Piece of rock which strikes metal to make a spark; this lights the gunpowder and fires the gun

DON QUIXOTE
Miguel de Cervantes, of Spain, wrote *Don Quixote* in the early 1600s. The novel tells of a foolish old man who jousts with windmills thinking they are giants and treats a peasant girl as his lady. He feels a sad yearning for lost knightly ideals and chivalry.

WHEEL-LOCK PISTOL
With better-quality gunpowder and larger numbers of soldiers being armed with guns, there was little place for the armored knight. Cuirassiers and light cavalry carried two wheel-lock pistols. This German example of about 1590 has an ebony stock inlaid with engraved panels and strips of stag's horn.

Key cylinder

Ramrod

Screwdriver

KEY
This German wrench of about 1620 wound up a spring on the wheel lock which, when released by the sear, or trigger, spun a wheel and lowered the lock against it, causing a shower of sparks to ignite the gunpowder.

Swivel eye for suspension

Pivoting pricker to unblock vent

This late-16th-century cartridge box was designed to hang from a belt

THE VICTOR
The chivalrous ideal knight is shown about to receive his prize on this Victorian silhouette. The knight in shining armor, the quest for the Holy Grail, and other legendary Arthurian adventures appealed to the romantic Victorian mind.

Index

Acknowledgments

DK would like to thank:

The authorities of the following castles and museums for permission to photograph and for providing objects for photography: Dover Castle, Hedingham Castle, Château de Loches, Marksburg, Pfalzgrafenstein, Château de Saumur; English Heritage, the National Trust, and CADW (Welsh Historical Monuments) for permission to photograph at Bodiam, Caerphilly, and Rochester Castles; the British Museum, especially the Department of Medieval and Later Antiquities; the Museum of London; the Museum of the Order of St. John; the Royal Armouries; The Wallace Collection; and The York Archaeological Trust for Excavation and Research Ltd.

For providing information and objects for photography: Richard Fitch and Mark Meltonville of Wolfbane; Peter and Joyce Butler, and Tracy Chadwick (medical herbalist) of Saxon Village Crafts; Anthony Barton, medieval musical instrument consultant; Bob Powell at the Weald and Downland Open Air Museum, Sussex; Steve Hollick and Chris Kemp, and all members of the National Guild of Stonemasons and Carvers, London; Caroline Benyon at Carl Edwards Studio; Jon Marrow at Norton Priory Museum Trust; the Dean and Chapter of York; All Saints Church, North Street, York; St. Nicholas Church, Stanford-on-Avon; and the Castle Museum Norwich, Norfolk Museums Service.

The Cotswold Farm Park for providing animals for photography. Alex Summers and the Order of the Black Prince for providing models and objects for photography; and the following people for acting as models: Penny Britchfield, Paul Cannings, Dorian Davies, Bob Dow, Paul Elliott, Ray Monery, Robin Pritchard, Jonathan Waller, and John Waller.

Angels, Burmans, and Nicki Sandford for costumes.
Anita Burger and Caroline Giles for hair and makeup.
David Edge for information and Plantagenet Somerset Fry for consultancy.

Susila Baybars and Helena Spiteri for editorial help; Joe Hoyle, Cormac Jordan, Manisha Patel, and Sharon Spencer for design assistance.

Additional photography: Peter Anderson (26c, 26bl, 102bc); John Chase (108cr); Steve Gorton (104–105c); Peter Hayman, Ivor Kerslake, and Nick Nichols (36c, 36l, 37bl, 48cr, 108 cl, 108bc); and Gary Ombler (100–101).

Model makers: Peter Griffiths and Gordon Models
Artwork: Joanna Cameron, Anna Ravenscroft, and John Woodcock

Indexer: Marion Dent
Assistant Editor: Joanne Matthews
Designer: Maggie Tingle

Picture credits
(l =left r=right t=top b=below c=center a=above f=front)

Aerofilms: 10bl, 15tl.
AKG, London: 6br, 100bc; /Photo: Erich Lessing/Galleria dell'Accademia, Florence 7c; /Pfarrkirche, Cappenberg 7bl; /Bern, Burgerbibliotheque 53tl; /Bibliotheque de Ste. Genevieve 37tl.
Ancient Art & Architecture Collection: 10cl, 18tl, 39bl, 104tr, 114cr, 118cl, 118c, 118tr, 119bl.
Ashmolean Museum, Oxford: 7c, 111bl.
Keith Barley: 107tl.
Bridgeman Art Library, London: /Biblioteca Estense, Modena 58b; /Bibliotheque Municipal de Lyon 85tr, 113c; Bibliotheque Nationale, Paris 12cr, 35tl, 42tr, 48tr, 59br, 63tr, 71tr, 72bl, 73t, 83tl, 84bl, 110tr, 111tc, 112bl, 115cl, 117tr; /Bibliotheque de la Sorbonne, Paris 6bl; /British Library, London: 7tc, 11cr, 21bl, 33br, 36tl, 37tr, 38br, 40cl, 41bl, 44br, 44bl, 46br, 48cl, 49cl, 51tl, 52tr, 54tr, 54br, 55tl, 67tc, 68tr,
68c, 79tr, 84tl, 96tr, 98b, 98c, 108br, 109cl, 111cl, 112tl; /With special authorisation of the City of Bayeux 7tl; /Corpus Christi College, Cambridge 61cr; Corpus Christi College, Oxford 112br; Department of the Environment, London 39tl; /Ecole des Beaux-Arts, Paris 28bl; /Fitzwilliam Museum, University of Cambridge 35bl, 41cl; /Galleria degli Uffizi, Florence 107br; /Giraudon/Musee Conde, Chantilly 36bc, 46tr, 80bl, 81bl; Kunsthistorisches Museum, Vienna 38bc; /Musée Conde, Chantilly 55br; /San Francesco Upper Church, Assissi 99tl; /Sixth Parish Church, Haut-Savoie, France 37br; /Trinity College, Dublin 6tr; /University of Oxford for the Bodleian Library 55cl, 87cl; /Vatican Library, Rome 41tl, 80br; /By Courtesy of the Board of Trustees of the Victoria & Albert Museum 21tc, 32tr; /Westminster Abbey, London 34tr; /Wrangham Collection 119c.
British Library, London: 27br.
British Museum, London: 35r, 36bl, 50cl, 96cl, 111tr.
Britstock-IFA: 10tr.
Bulloz/Ecole des Beaux-Arts, Paris: 29tc.
Burgerbibliothek, Bern: 83cr.
Jean-Loup Charmet, Paris: 103tl, 108tr.
Danish National Museum, Copenhagen: 6c.
E.T. Archive: 8bl, 30tr, 30br, 38ac, 43tc, 59tl, 66bl, 71c, 79bl, 85cl, 88cr, 89tl, 89bc, 92bl, 93bl, 95cl, 95cr, 106tl, 117bc, 118cr, 119cl, 122cl, 122tr; /Biblioteca Augustea, Perugia 27tr; /Biblioteca Marciana 48bl; /Biblioteca Estense, Modena 100c; /Bibliotheque Nationale, Paris 42cl; /British Library, London 40tr, 67bc, 94c; /Fitzwilliam Museum, Cambridge 78cr; /Victoria & Albert Museum, London 45br, 45cr.
Mary Evans Picture Library: 24cr, 38tr.
Werner Forman Archive, London: /Boston Museum of Fine Arts 121br; Burke Collection, New York 120tl; /Kita-In, Saitumi 120c; /Metropolitan Museum of Art, New York 111br; /Museum of Catalan Art, Barcelona 23tl.
Photographie Giraudon/Bibliotheque Nationale, Paris: 32tl.
Sonia Halliday & Laura Lushington Photographs: /Victoria & Albert Museum, London 46c.
Sonia Halliday Photographs: 107c.
Robert Harding Picture Library: 7br, 12bl, 14cl, 16cl, 17tc, 34br, 56br, 56bl, 60cr, 66tr, 86b, 86tl, 87tl, 102br, 105tl, 113bl, 115t; /British Library 56cl, 59cl, 74b, 75bl; /British Museum 16tr.
Michael Holford: 14tr, 22–23, 22tl, 40bl, 113br, 120bl.
Hulton-Deutsch Collection: 116cl.
Mark MacLoskey: 10–11.
Mansell Collection: 59bl, 69cl, 76br, 113tl, 122tl, 125bl; /Alinari 76tr.
Bildarchiv Foto Marburg: 78br.
Arxiu Mas: 112cl.
Musee des Arts Decoratifs, Paris/Photo: Sully-Jaulmes: 40c.
Museum of London: 26bc.
Osterreichische Nationalbibliotehek, Vienna (Cod. 2597, f.15): 70br.
Pierpont Morgan Library, New York: 91c.
Puffin Books: Churches & Cathedrals by Helen Leacroft, 1957. Reproduced by permission of Penguin Books Ltd: 105tr, 105cr.
Scala, Florence: 9br, 56tcl, 95t; /Archivo di Stato, Siena 32cl.
Sir John Soane's Museum, London: 105br.
Stadtbibliothek Nurnberg: 65cr.
Stiftsbibliothek St. Gallen: 8c.
Syndication International: 23tr, 71tl, 80tr, 94bc, 117tl; /British Museum 96tl.
Trinity College Library, Cambridge: 101tr.
Courtesy of the Board of Trustees of the Victoria & Albert Museum: 112b.
Wallace Collection: 39tr.
ZEFA: 23cr, 24tr, 123tl.
Jacket: Sonia Halliday photography: fcl; Eg 1070 f.4v Coat of Arms of Rene, Duke of Anjou (1409–80), Book of Hours or Rene Anjou (15th century), British Library, London / Bridgeman Art Library, London / New York: fc.

Every effort has been made to trace the copyright holders of photographs. The publisher apologizes for any unintentional omissions and would be pleased, in such cases, to amend future editions.